STUDIES IN FRENCH

General
W. G. M

For Jenny, Tony and Loraine

CAMUS:
L'ETRANGER

by

G. V. BANKS

Lecturer in French, University of Birmingham

EDWARD ARNOLD

First published 1976 by
Edward Arnold (Publishers) Ltd
41 Bedford Square, London WC1B 3DQ

Reprinted 1978, 1981, 1982

ISBN: 0 7131 5850 6

Printed and bound in Great Britain at
The Camelot Press Ltd, Southampton

Contents

Note

Given the scope of this essay, I have made no mention of other critics within it. Yet I have benefited greatly from many works devoted to Camus and *L'Etranger*. I take this opportunity of expressing my indebtedness to these writers and of apologizing for my apparent failure to recognize their work. I hope the select critical bibliography, in which they all appear, makes some amends.

Quotations from and page references to *L'Etranger* are taken throughout from the Folio edition (Paris, Gallimard, copyright 1957, reprinted 1972). I have adopted the following system of reference: page 129 of Chapter III, Part II appears as (II, III.129) and so on.

References to other works by Camus are taken from the NRF Pléiade editions of Camus's works (*Théâtre, Récits, Nouvelles*, Paris, Gallimard, 1962, and *Essais*, Paris, Gallimard 1965).

The works in question are referred to in abbreviated form as follows: *L'Envers et l'endroit*: (EE); *Noces*: (N); *Le Mythe de Sisyphe*: (MS); *L'Intelligence et l'échafaud*: (IE).

1. Introduction

First published in 1942, *L'Etranger* continues to excite many who read and re-read it. In writing it Camus found the literary medium best suited to his talents. For the lasting popularity and reputation of this essayist, dramatist, novelist, moralist and polemicist rest mainly upon his works of imaginative prose fiction: *L'Etranger* (1942), *La Peste* (1947), *La Chute* (1956), *L'Exil et le royaume* (1957). In these four works, varied though they may be in style and tone, Camus explores and exploits the single voice, the single consciousness; in each of them he creates a central fictional character grappling with the implications of human existence in an apparently absurd world. *L'Etranger*, the first of these works, is perhaps the most accomplished and compelling of them.

It is the work of a young author, on the threshold of what turned out to be a distinguished and prematurely ended literary career. (He was killed in a car crash in 1960 at the age of forty-six.) Abandoning his unfinished novel *La Mort heureuse*, in which the principal character Mersault may be seen in some ways as the prototype of Meursault, Camus began work on *L'Etranger* in 1938. He completed it in May 1940 at the age of twenty-six. This cool, elegant and startling book is the creation of an author living in a precarious present and uncertain of his future.

For Camus's early years as a writer (1935–42) are years of restless, even somewhat feverish activity. His interests are many, his energy boundless. His personal life (a broken marriage, a second marriage, a serious illness, considerable penury); his political life (his support for the Algerian Arabs' demands for social justice, for the republican cause in the Spanish Civil War, his eventual joining of the French Resistance); his professional life (his débuts as literary critic, journalist, political commentator); his life in the theatre (principal founder and director of, and actor in the *Théâtre du Travail*, then the *Théâtre de L'Equipe*); his intellectual life (the reading of Nietzsche, Kierkegaard, Dostoievski, Kafka, Gide, Malraux, Sartre); his acutely sensitive reaction to his environment (a sharp awareness of the natural beauty of Algeria and the poverty and wretchedness of many of the people living there), all suggest that considerable demands—

intellectual, emotional and physical—are made upon him throughout these years.

His literary output during this period is considerable. As well as *L'Etranger*, he writes the essays *L'Envers et l'endroit*, *Noces*, and *Le Mythe de Sisyphe*, the novel *La Mort heureuse* and the play *Caligula*. In their different ways these works all reflect Camus's preoccupation with what he calls *une sensibilité absurde*.

This *sensibilité absurde* informs *L'Etranger* to a considerable degree. An account of Camus's conception of the Absurd and its implications therefore forms a part of this study. But its relevance to the novel must be kept in perspective. *L'Etranger* is a creative work of imaginative prose fiction, and not the mere literary counterpart and reiteration of a collection of essays on the 'philosophy of the Absurd'. Furthermore, it is inappropriate to apply the word philosophy to Camus's deliberations on the Absurd; at the time of writing *L'Etranger* he makes his attitude clear on this matter. In a preface to his celebrated essays on the Absurd, *Le Mythe de Sisyphe*, published in 1942, he writes:

> Les pages qui suivent traitent d'une sensibilité absurde qu'on peut trouver éparse dans le siècle—et non d'une philosophie absurde que notre temps, à proprement parler, n'a pas connue. . . . On trouvera seulement ici la description, à l'état pur, d'un mal de l'esprit. Aucune métaphysique, aucune croyance n'y sont mêlées pour le moment. (*MS*,97)

L'Etranger is the story of a French Algerian clerk named Meursault who kills an Arab, and is imprisoned, tried and condemned to death for having done so. Within this simple framework Camus presents a character who fascinates and disturbs us, one who 'refuses to play the social game, who refuses to lie, who agrees to die for the truth as he sees it.' It is also a critique: a critique of capital punishment and of the legal system which condones it, of a whole system of social, moral and religious values, of complacency, of men who believe that they have understood and can explain the meaning of life, of men who believe that they have the right to judge others.

In imagining Meursault, Camus creates a character who assumes the proportions of a modern myth, a character imbued with that *sensibilité absurde éparse dans le siècle* and archetypally representative of it. Meursault is the mythical incarnation of the belief which Ionesco expresses thus:

> Aucune société n'a pu abolir la tristesse humaine, aucun système politique ne peut nous libérer de la douleur de vivre, de la peur de mourir, de notre soif de

l'absolu. C'est la condition humaine qui gouverne la condition sociale, non le contraire. (*Notes et contre-notes*, Paris, Gallimard 1962)

Above all else, Camus is an artist: 'Pourquoi suis-je un artiste et non un philosophe? C'est que je pense selon les mots et non selon les idées' (*Carnets* 1945). Above all else *L'Etranger* is a work of literature, and it is as such that this essay considers it.

2. The Récit: Experience and Reflection

I

Le roman refabrique un univers dans sa complexité et sa durée.   Quilliot

The narrative form of *L'Etranger*, a relatively short work of prose fiction written in the first person, is one of considerable importance in the development of French literature. Works such as Prévost's *Manon Lescaut*, Constant's *Adolphe*, Gide's *La Symphonie pastorale*, Sartre's *La Nausée*, varied though they are in historical moment, in tone, in moral and philosophical intention, belong to the same tradition.

Given the particular narrative form these works share, they all pose crucial questions concerning the relationship of the author to his character-narrator: to what extent does the author identify with his character-narrator, to what extent is he different from him? To what degree does the author criticize his character, to what degree sympathize with him? How representative of the author's own ideas, attitudes and experiences are those of his character? Why does the author choose to present his character in a medium which, ostensibly at least, allows him to tell his own story? What advantages are to be gained from opting for the first person narrative, a technique in some ways more limiting than its conventional alternative, the third person narrative? No single solution ever offers itself in answer to these questions, for the relationship is always a complex one.

It is a particular characteristic of *L'Etranger* that, however many times we read it, we are all too prone to forget that Camus, not Meursault, wrote it. This in itself is a tribute to Camus's narrative art, for the illusion achieved is deliberate on his part. Vividly, self-effacingly, he creates his

character's world and persuades us, irresistibly, to live in it. But Camus is
the artist, Meursault his fictional creation.

Camus called *L'Etranger* a *roman*. However, it has become fairly
common practice on the part of critics to describe Camus's *L'Etranger*
more specifically as a *récit*; to speak, for example, when discussing it of
'l'art du récit'.

Camus admired André Gide and it is to his work that we turn, notably
to *L'Immoraliste* (1902), *La Porte étroite* (1909), *La Symphonie pastorale*
(1919), to illustrate the essential characteristics of the *récit*, for he is its
principal and most influential exponent. Camus makes clear his debt to
Gide:

> C'est à l'artiste surtout qu'allait mon culte, au maître du classicisme moderne,
> disons au Gide des *Prétextes*. Connaissant bien l'anarchie de ma nature, j'ai
> besoin de me donner en art des barrières. Gide m'a appris à le faire. Sa
> conception du classicisme considéré comme un romantisme dompté est la
> mienne.

The Gidean *récit* is compressed, concentrated, economically expressed.
It is somewhat shorter than the average novel, considerably longer than
the average short story. The first person narrator dominates the entire
work. It is he who is at once the experiencer, the witness and the narrator
of the events described. So the *récit* is based upon the tone of the single
voice, the exploration of the single consciousness, the description of the
single existence at grips with the world of experience. The events
described in the *récit* are in the nature of some form of crisis in the life of
the narrator, a crisis of such proportions that it shapes and determines his
destiny. In the Gidean *récit*, whether it takes the form of a simple written
account, or of a monologue delivered to friends, or of an edited diary, the
dénouement, the outcome of this crisis, has already taken place; the
narrator's destiny has already been shaped and determined. Thus the
narrator's account of his emotional and moral crisis and its result is a
retrospective recreation of experience undergone. We have then a
narrative viewpoint allowing for a detailed and precise analysis and an
illumination of behaviour, motivation and feelings.

Gide never intervenes *directly* in the narrative. At first sight the
character is given the freedom to tell his story in what he would like us to
believe is an objective manner. But through the art of indirect
insinuation, Gide demonstrates that his character's 'objectivity' is a
pseudo-objectivity, that his viewpoint is a partial and subjective one.

And the character's narrative 'freedom' is a specious freedom. Singularly lacking a sense of humour, a sense of irony and self-irony, Gide's character-narrators are the victims of the author's sense of humour and irony. Frequently in sympathy with them, at times even seeming to identify with them, Gide ultimately distances himself from his characters. He makes his olympian presence felt within the narrative.

Certain similarities between the Gidean *récit* and Camus's *L'Etranger* may be noted. The style of *L'Etranger* is compressed, concentrated, economic. It is the story of a single individual at grips with the world of experience, the exploration of a single consciousness, the sound of a single voice. Meursault experiences, Meursault witnesses, Meursault narrates. The other characters, to varying degrees but without exception, are of strictly minor importance. They are seen through Meursault's eyes, described from his point of view, and achieve significance in so far as they reflect an aspect of his experience and contribute to his destiny. And Meursault's destiny is the subject proper of *L'Etranger*. The events which constitute the matter of the *récit*: events such as his mother's death, the smoking of a cigarette, the murder of an Arab, writing a letter, taking a swim, being tried and condemned to death, events great and small encompass, in their profusion and totality, a crisis in the life of the narrator. It is a crisis of such proportions that, in a very stark sense, it shapes and determines Meursault's destiny.

But beyond this point the differences between the Gidean *récit* and *L'Etranger* are what strike us as important. Where the narrative technique of *L'Etranger* and its implications are concerned, they provoke more questions than the similarities. If the Gidean *récit* takes the form of a retrospective recreation and analysis of an experience already completed, can we say the same in the case of Meursault's account of his experience? Where *L'Etranger* is concerned we are led to ask: is the narrative the retrospective account, the considered recreation of a crisis and its outcome? Or is it rather in the form of a diary, the immediate or near-immediate recording of events as and when they occur? There are, as we shall see, arguments both for and against either proposition. But the *récit* cannot be both; our view of Meursault, our interpretation of the book must hinge to a considerable degree upon the conclusion we draw.

Further, the process of psychological analysis of behaviour, motivation and feelings which plays such an important part in the Gidean *récit* is, ostensibly at least, totally lacking within the fabric of Meursault's narration. Indeed we can go so far as to say that, in Meursault, Camus creates a character who has as one of his principal characteristics the refusal at all times—often in the face of considerable pressure from the *comparses*—to indulge, for them or for us, in any such exercise. Perhaps above all other things the exploration and analysis of his own or other people's motivations and feelings seem to be anathema to Camus's character-narrator. Is the dominant narrative tone of *L'Etranger* not rather based upon a flat, dispassionate description of people and events, deliberately avoiding the slightest attempt at analysis, understanding and interpretation either of the self or of others? Yet, paradoxically perhaps, the 'psychology' of Meursault has always held, and perhaps always will hold, a particular fascination for a great number of critics and readers.

Moreover, with regard to authorial narrative viewpoint *L'Etranger* conveys a very different impression from that found in the Gidean *récit*. For if authorial intervention on the part of Gide is never direct, it is nevertheless, in an indirect, insinuating way, manifestly present within the texture of the narrative. But to all appearances Camus never intrudes in any way. The suspension of disbelief in the authenticity of Meursault's tale is never broken, its 'objectivity' never (ostensibly) questioned. Meursault is apparently given unhindered freedom to tell us his own story, to persuade us of its truth. Where then is Camus?

'Personnalité de l'auteur absente', says Flaubert in speaking of his own narrative role in the novel *Madame Bovary*, an assertion laying claim to a certain objectivity, to an authorial absence or withdrawal granting freedom of action and expression to his characters, freedom of opinion and interpretation to his readers. But such an aim, even given sincerity of intention on the part of the author, is surely impossible to fulfil. The style of *Madame Bovary*—of any work of art—is necessarily a function of the personality, of the vision of the author; Flaubert is ever-present. So it is with Camus and *L'Etranger*. It is not a question of *intervention*, direct or indirect. Such interventions are non-existent. Meursault tells his story unhampered by his creator and the reader enters into direct and uninterrupted relationship with him. On this level Camus is 'absent' from the work. But on another, deeper level—the level dictated by the very process of creating imaginative fiction—he is always there.

Meursault is 'l'étranger'; he and *L'Etranger* are one and indivisible. Meursault, apparently so simple, straightforward, transparent, is revealed on closer acquaintance to be complex, ambiguous, subject to inner tensions. So it is with the style of *L'Etranger*. A deceptive surface of simplicity and ease concealing complexities, ambiguities and tensions is an essential quality, perhaps the very essence of Camus's art in the *récit*.

L'Etranger is a carefully structured, tightly-woven novel in which nothing is gratuitous. Its structure is strikingly symmetrical, its two parts being of almost exactly equal length. (The six chapters of Part I cover some eighty-five pages, the five chapters of Part II some eighty-eight). Beneath this basic division of the novel into two parts we detect a further symmetrical structure of a thematic nature, a structuring of the chapter divisions into the pattern 5–1–5. Within this pattern Chapter VI of Part I plays a central and pivotal role. It is an account of the Sunday on which Meursault kills the Arab and a description of the killing. On one level it belongs to Part I, is its climax and conclusion; on another, that concerning death, one of the book's central themes, it serves as a link between Part I (Chapters I-V) and Part II. For the substance of the *récit* is organized within the framework of three deaths. It opens with a death (that of Meursault's mother); it closes with a death (Meursault facing and reflecting on his own imminent execution); it has as its central pivot, both thematically and structurally, a death (that of the Arab). Chapters 1–5 of Part I are an account of events leading up to the murder. Part II is a reconsideration of those events and the description of their consequences.

Whilst Parts I and II are closely similar in length, they are strikingly different in their treatment of time, in the time spans they encompass. Part I covers a period of some eighteen days in Meursault's life, Part II a period of about a year. In neither Part is any attempt made to treat the passage of time and Meursault's experience of it in an even or comprehensive manner. The *récit* is in no way a blow by blow account, as it were, of every detail of his daily life. On the contrary, whatever our initial impression, a relatively small number of incidents and experiences form the substance of the *récit*; time and experience in time are treated in a highly selective and subjective manner.

The six chapters of Part I which cover the eighteen days beginning with the news of the death of Meursault's mother and ending with the death of the Arab are made up as follows: Chapter I—a day and a half. Meursault learns of his mother's death, travels to the *asile*, attends the vigil and the burial, returns to Algiers. Chapter II—two days (Saturday and Sunday). Meursault goes swimming, meets Marie, takes her to the cinema, sleeps with her. Sunday he spends in his apartment or on its balcony watching the world go by. Chapter III—one day; Meursault tells us he works hard and well at the office. A swim and lunch with his friend Emmanuel. The evening is spent first with Salamano; we learn of him and his dog. Then with Raymond; we are given an account of his relationship with his mistress. Meursault writes the letter for him. Chapter IV—two days (Saturday and Sunday; by far the greater part taken up with description of Sunday). Meursault spends Saturday on the beach with Marie. She stays the night, spends Sunday morning with Meursault, leaves him at midday after they have witnessed Raymond's brawl with his mistress and his confrontation with the policeman. Meursault and Raymond spend the afternoon and early evening together. Meursault agrees to act as witness for him in his 'affair'. They meet Salamano who, we learn in some detail, has lost his dog. Chapter V—one day. Raymond invites Meursault and Marie to spend Sunday with Masson. Meursault's boss offers him promotion (which he refuses), Marie offers him marriage (which he seems to accept). He dines at Celeste's, is fascinated by the automaton-lady. The late evening is spent in a long conversation with Salamano about his dog and Meursault's mother. Chapter VI—half a day. The morning on the beach, early lunch at Masson's, the confrontations with the Arabs, the murder in mid-afternoon. Thus only eight of the eighteen days in question are dealt with to any degree of significance at all within the narrative. More important, only certain specific events occurring within those days are highlighted. The detailed and prolonged descriptions of the numerous conversations with Raymond and Salamano, of the vigil, of the funeral procession, of the walk along the beach towards the Arab, go to make up a proportion of the substance of Part I sharply contrasting with the proportion of the *objective* time they represent within the eighteen days comprising the overall time-span of Part I, or indeed of the eight days contained within the narrative.

The implications of this are twofold. First, those encounters and events in Part I which emerge to dominate the description of experience undergone, which are dwelt upon at a length and in a manner making a deep impression upon the reader, do so because, *in the light of Meursault's experience related in Part II*, they come to assume a crucial significance. Despite appearances, there is nothing arbitrary, gratuitous, or coincidental about the content of Part I. It is the result of a careful process of selection and organization on the part of Camus.

Secondly, to create in the reader a sense of immediacy, an impression of sharing experience lived and recounted in the near or immediate present is one of Camus's fundamental intentions in Part I of the *récit*. And a sense of immediacy is, overwhelmingly, its dominant feature. Meursault's experience of life in the present is, like anyone's experience of life in the present, imbued with an impression of apparent shapelessness, contingency and haphazardness. To yesterday, to last year we can give a shape and a meaning (however selective and subjective); to tomorrow, to next year we can give a shape and meaning (however hypothetical and idealized).

Only in retrospect can we recognize those events which were instrumental in shaping our lives—they may have seemed quite without significance at the time; only with hindsight can we determine those events which had little or no bearing on our future—they may have seemed of enormous importance at the time. Today, the *now* of our experience is, till it is past, beyond our powers of understanding or categorization. Thus, in pursuit of his intention, Camus presents us with a series of todays. Our initial impression of Meursault's experience in Part I is that of life lived in a series of instant presents, of a profusion and confusion of events which are fragmented, disjointed, seemingly devoid of all causality and consequence.

The opening words of each chapter convey this sense of the present and establish the temporal framework within which the narrative moves. The first three chapters all contain the word *aujourd'hui* within the first sentence: 'Aujourd'hui maman est morte' (9); 'En me réveillant, j'ai compris pourquoi mon patron avait l'air mécontent quand je lui ai demandé mes deux jours de congé: c'est aujourd'hui samedi' (33); 'Aujourd'hui j'ai beaucoup travaillé au bureau' (43). The openings of the following three chapters, whilst they are less specific and indicate in fact a certain widening of the temporal perspective, nevertheless convey, in their different ways, the same air of immediacy: 'J'ai bien travaillé toute la semaine, Raymond est venu et m'a dit qu'il avait envoyé la lettre. . . . Hier c'était samedi. . . .' (57); 'Raymond m'a téléphoné au bureau. Il m'a dit qu'un de ses amis (il lui avait parlé de moi) m'invitait à passer la journée de dimanche dans son cabanon, près d'Alger' (67); 'Le dimanche j'ai eu de la peine à me réveiller et il a fallu que Marie m'appelle et me secoue' (77).

Throughout Part I the use of tenses lends further weight to the impression that we are sharing Meursault's experience in the immediate or near present. In this respect the justly famous opening of the narrative is something of a *tour de force*.

Aujourd'hui maman est morte. Ou peut-être hier, je ne sais pas. J'ai reçu un télégramme de l'asile: 'Mère décédée. Enterrement demain. Sentiments distingués'. Cela ne veut rien dire. C'était peut-être hier.

L'asile de vieillards est à Marengo, à quatre-vingts kilomètres d'Alger. Je prendrai l'autobus à deux heures et j'arriverai dans l'après-midi. Ainsi je pourrai veiller et je rentrerai demain soir. J'ai demandé deux jours de congé à mon patron et il ne pouvait pas me les refuser avec une excuse pareille. Mais il n'avait pas l'air content. . . . C'était plutôt à lui de me présenter ses condoléances. Mais il le fera après-demain sans doute quand il me verra en deuil. Pour le moment c'est un peu comme si maman n'était pas morte. Après l'enterrement, au contraire, ce sera une affaire classée et tout aura revêtu une allure plus officielle.

J'ai pris l'autobus à deux heures. Il faisait très chaud. J'ai mangé au restaurant, chez Céleste, comme d'habitude. (I.I, 9–10)

Only in the third paragraph does the narrative settle to a consistent use of the tenses in which the *récit* is principally written: namely the perfect and imperfect tenses. Even then the sense of immediacy persists. Above all, the opening paragraphs of the novel, in which the perfect, the present, the imperfect and the future tenses are fused, convey to us most vividly the impression of an experience now being lived and the instantaneous recording of that experience. We are thrown immediately into Meursault's present and into the 'presentness' of his account of it. Throughout Part I the manipulation of the sequence of tenses continues to be a major means of creating the illusion of immediacy.

In absolute terms, experience of the indivisibly immediate present can never be fully translated into written form. This is a feature which informs the philosophic and aesthetic preoccupations of Sartre in *La Nausée*, and which is also hauntingly present throughout the work of Beckett. Experience and the formulation of experience can never be completely simultaneous. Even if one uses the present tense to record experience, that present tense cannot be the *present* of the lived experience; it can only be a literary device—albeit at times a most effective and convincing one—used to give a sense of 'presentness' to what must, by definition, be experience in the past (however immediate). Even so, if Camus's *sole* intention in Part I were to create the illusion of the immediate present, the use of the present tense as the basic narrative tense might seem best suited to that purpose.

But in *L'Etranger* the creation of the illusion of immediacy is only half the story. Camus's intentions are twofold. For allied to the notion of immediacy of experience and its narration is the notion of a considered, retrospective account of experience already completed. The basic narrative tense he employs, the perfect tense, is ideally suited to this dual intention. The perfect tense ('Aujourd'hui maman est morte') is less distant, less formal than its companion past tense, the past definite ('Aujourd'hui maman mourut').

The past definite is the more usual and conventional past tense employed in literature; it is more literary in that it emphasizes the composed and considered nature of what is written, in a sense more 'past' as it confers on the events described, both in their detail and within an overall pattern, a certain finality. But the general tone of L'Etranger is often, though not always, wilfully unliterary; it is informal, familiar, intimate. The perfect tense belongs to this general tone. It is the usual tense identified with spoken French, with the living word, with the vitality and muscularity of language in action. One of its parts, the auxiliary, is a present form, the present form of one of those two most familiar and everyday verbs être and avoir, a fact which in a very basic visual as well as auditory sense introduces into the expression used an element of presentness. (Does 'Aujourd'hui maman est morte' really convey a sense of the past?) So, whilst it is a past tense, it may create an impression of the present, may hold for us, emotionally and psychologically, much of the value of the present tense. And this is how it functions frequently in L'Etranger; it is used to describe events which have taken place in the past in a way which endows them, in the eyes of the reader, with the value and the texture of a present.

As is the case in Part I, much of Part II is taken up with the detailed description of certain specific events. Again, the space and attention accorded to these events is out of all proportion to the time they actually take to unfold within the twelve-month period which is the temporal framework of Part II. Chapter I comprises accounts of the first meeting with the *juge d'instruction*, the interview with the *avocat*, and, finally, the description, couched in vivid and dramatic terms, of the crucial confrontation with the *juge d'instruction*. Chapter II (114–19) recounts Marie's visit to Meursault in prison. Chapters III and IV are a detailed description of the trial and condemnation. Chapter V contains an account of the *aumônier*'s visit and of Meursault's violent reaction to him. This final chapter closes with a description of Meursault's state of mind as his story ends. These several events, covering at most in their totality a period of some five or six days, account for by far the greater part of the narrative. So once more in Part II no attempt at an overall description of the passage of objective time is made; a small number of crucial encounters and experiences are highlighted in Meursault's consciousness and memory of the period involved. Thus they dominate his *récit*.

Yet, whilst in Part I the time dimension explored expands very rarely indeed beyond that of the immediate or near-immediate present, within the substance of the narrative of Part II it expands considerably.

We have noted the importance of the chapter openings in Part I; they establish impressively the time scale within which the narrative is to move. The same technique is employed in Part II but to quite different ends; the impression made upon the reader contrasts fundamentally with that made in Part I:

> Tout de suite après mon arrestation, j'ai été interrogé plusieurs fois. Mais il s'agissait d'interrogatoires d'identité qui n'ont pas duré longtemps. La première fois au commissariat mon affaire semblait n'intéresser personne. Huit jours après, le juge d'instruction, au contraire, m'a regardé avec curiosité. (II.I, 99)

The chapter ends thus:

> Et au bout des onze mois qu'a duré cette instruction, je peux dire que je m'étonnais presque de m'être réjoui d'autre chose que de ces rares instants où le juge me reconduisait à la porte de son cabinet en me frappant sur l'épaule et en me disant d'un air cordial: 'C'est fini pour aujourd'hui, monsieur l'Antéchrist'. On me remettait alors entre les mains des gendarmes. (110–111)

Chapter II begins:

> Il y a des choses dont je n'ai jamais aimé parler. Quand je suis entré en prison, j'ai compris au bout de quelques jours que je n'aimerais pas parler de cette partie de ma vie.
> Plus tard je n'ai plus trouvé d'importance à ces répugnances. En réalité, je n'étais pas réellement en prison les premiers jours: j'attendais vaguement quelque événement nouveau. C'est seulement après la première et la seule visite de Marie que tout a commencé. (II.II, 113)

The chapter ends:

> Mais en même temps et pour la première fois depuis bien des mois, j'ai entendu distinctement le son de ma voix. Je l'ai reconnu pour celle qui résonnait déjà depuis de longs jours à mes oreilles et j'ai compris que pendant tout ce temps j'avais parlé seul. . . . Non, il n'y avait pas d'issue et personne ne peut imaginer ce que sont les soirs dans les prisons. (126–7)

Chapter III begins:

> Je peux dire, qu'au fond l'été a très vite remplacé l'été. (II.III, 129)

Chapter V begins:

> Pour la troisième fois j'ai refusé de voir l'aumônier.   (II.V, 167)

It is clear that, in organizing the openings and closings of the chapters in this way, Camus wishes to impress upon the reader that, notwithstanding the apparent immediacy of much of the narrative, Meursault's account of his experience from the time of his arrest till the time of his condemnation is a retrospective one, embarked upon after the completion of the events described. His *récit* is the result of a period of reflection.

To a considerable degree the narrative tone of Part II is also that of an exercise in reflection. Chapter II is perhaps the most obvious illustration of this point. Following the detailed account of Marie's visit (114–19), the rest of the chapter—well over half of it—embraces more or less the whole period of Meursault's imprisonment. In a contemplative vein he discusses the several months when he still has 'des pensées d'homme libre', the gradual way in which over a period of several months he learned to do without the company of women (Marie and others), and without cigarettes (Part I makes it clear that he is a heavy smoker, especially in moments of stress); how, after bouts of insomnia during the early stages of his imprisonment, he eventually became able to sleep sixteen to eighteen hours a day; how, most important of all, he learned to remember his past life as a means of killing time. He becomes accustomed to his imprisonment ('C'était d'ailleurs une idée de maman, et elle le répétait souvent, qu'on finissait par s'habituer à tout' (120)), and in the process undergoes a loss of a sense of time.

This mode of existence, where contemplation comes to replace activity, is further exemplified in the first half of the final chapter.

The first ten pages of Chapter V (167–77) do nothing to advance the narrative. Apart from the ensuing visit of the *aumônier* the story is now complete. Meursault reflects. His moods oscillate from hope to despair; hope of a pardon, despair at the impossibility of escaping the 'mécanisme implacable' consequent upon his condemnation to death. He reflects upon execution in general, the arbitrary nature of his own sentence, upon the possibility of reforming the law, upon the shape of the guillotine. He recalls his father vomiting after seeing a public execution, he remembers Marie. He is at once stoically resigned to the inevitability of his death and appalled at the thought of it:

> Dans le fond, je n'ignorais que mourir à trente ans ou à soixante-dix ans importe peu puisque, naturellement, dans les deux cas, d'autres hommes et d'autres femmes vivront, et cela pendant des milliers d'années. Rien n'était plus clair, en somme. C'était toujours moi qui mourrais, que ce soit maintenant ou dans vingt ans. A ce moment, ce qui gênait un peu dans mon raisonnement, c'était ce bond terrible que je sentais en moi à la pensée de vingt ans de vie à venir. (II.V, 175–6).

The content of this opening section of the final chapter, born of Meursault's reflections upon the events which have befallen him and the destiny which awaits him, grows to achieve the dimensions of a generalized and abstract contemplation of the arbitrary and absurd nature of our existence in time, of our finite and mortal individual lives measured against the vastness of the ages, the imponderable and inconceivable notion of eternity. As Pozzo puts it in Beckett's *En attendant Godot*: 'Elles accouchent à cheval sur une tombe; le jour brille un instant, puis c'est la nuit à nouveau.'

The detail, the mood, the overall structure of Part II of the *récit*, all suggest that it is the retrospective account of an experience already completed, the re-creation and reappraisal of a critical period in the life of the character-narrator. So, in a less obvious way, is Part I.

Despite the overwhelming sense of immediacy initially conveyed by the narrative style of Part I, the impression of a considered reappraisal of experience is at times strong:

> J'avais même l'impression que cette morte, couchée au milieu d'eux, ne signifiait rien à leurs yeux. Mais je crois maintenant que c'était une impression fausse. (I.I, 21)

Both the switch from the pluperfect tense to the present tense and the clearcut nature of the comment made about his earlier impression suggest a considerable lapse of time between the moment of experience and the moment of its being recorded. Meursault remembers:

> Tout s'est passé ensuite avec tant de précipitation, de certitude et de naturel, que je ne me souviens plus de rien. Une chose seulement: à l'entrée du village l'infirmière déléguée m'a parlé. Elle avait une voix singulière qui n'allait pas avec son visage, une voix mélodieuse et tremblante. Elle m'a dit: 'Si on va doucement on risque une insolation. Mais si on va trop vite, on est en transpiration et dans l'église on attrape un chaud et froid'. Elle avait raison. Il n'y avait pas d'issue. J'ai encore gardé quelques images de cette journée. . . . (I.I, 30–31)

The real present of this narrative, one during which the memory operates to reassemble the *images* retained of the funeral procession, is considerably removed in time from the events described.

Above all, let us turn to the closing passage of Chapter VI:

> La gachette a cédé, j'ai touché le ventre poli de la crosse et c'est là, dans le bruit à la fois sec et assourdissant que tout a commencé. J'ai secoué la sueur et le soleil. J'ai compris que j'avais détruit l'équilibre du jour, le silence exceptionnel d'une plage où j'avais été heureux. Alors, j'ai tiré encore quatre fois sur un corps inerte où les balles s'enfonçaient sans qu'il y parût. Et c'était comme quatre coups brefs que je frappais sur la porte du malheur.   (I.VI, 95)

That final melodramatic sentence—and for that matter: 'c'est là . . . que tout a commencé'—can surely only have been written by a narrator already aware of the consequences of his act. Overall this passage presents us, in concentrated form, with a Meursault moving from a state of unawareness through a stage of the intuitive, instinctive dawning of awareness of the implications of his act to a final state of full awareness of its consequences—a microcosmic illustration of the evolution in the levels of his consciousness contained within the general structure of the *récit*. Only the Meursault of stage three can have composed the account.

If the events described in detail in Part I are recorded before the principal events of Part II—the imprisonment, the trial, the condemnation—have taken place, then the relationship between the contents of the two parts rests upon a series of unconvincing coincidences. Suspending for a moment a concern with authorial intention, and working on the level of the internal *vraisemblance* of the narrative, it would indeed be strange if the detail of events related in an already-composed Part I turned to to be precisely reflected in the substance of the cross-examination Meursault undergoes in his trial. The substance of this cross-examination, the meat of the prosecution's case as it were, comprises, in large measure, an exploration and interpretation of Meursault's relationship with his mother and his behaviour during the time of the vigil and the burial, of his involvement with Marie and Raymond and, to some degree, the circumstances within which he murders the Arab and his motivation for doing so. As we have seen, within the eighteen days covered in Part I, a period described impressionistically, subjectively and selectively, these same events and experiences form by far the greater part of the narrative. They are exclusively—together with the portrait of Salamano and his dog—the subject of Part I.

Further, the characters appearing in Part I, in varying degrees of importance, are the only ones mentioned specifically as witnesses and observers at the trial:

> Du sein de ce public tout à l'heure informe, j'ai vu se lever un à un, pour disparaître ensuite par une porte latérale, le directeur et le concierge de l'asile, le vieux Thomas Pérez, Raymond, Masson, Salamano, Marie . . . à l'appel de son nom, le dernier, Céleste, s'est levé. J'ai reconnu à côté de lui la petite bonne femme du restaurant, avec sa jaquette et son air précis et décidé. Elle me regardait avec intensité.   (II.III, 135)

With the exception of *la petite bonne femme*—and how striking it is to find her mentioned in this company—these characters are called to witness. We know something of them all because of the content of Part I. But why them and only them?

The shift from a time span of eighteen days in Part I to that of a year in Part II, and the change in narrative tone which accompanies this shift derive naturally from and are perfectly suited to the radical alteration in Meursault's circumstances. The Meursault we encounter in Part I is free to live as he chooses. Not given to thought or reflection, caring little if at all for the past or the future—hardly the sort of man to keep a diary—he lives instinctively and spontaneously in and for the present. Hence the narrative style of Part I; it is vivid, immediate, spontaneous, built on the description of a series of immediate presents. The Meursault of Part II is imprisoned. His activities are curtailed, he has time—twelve months of time—on his hands. Consequently, and quite naturally, memory, reflection and contemplation become the principal modes of his existence. Into this new form of existence, largely the experience of solitary confinement, the trial itself intrudes in a bewildering manner. For two days Meursault, now solitary and withdrawn from the world, finds himself in an enclosed room where the heat is intense, the light glaring. The centre of attention, surrounded by journalists, spectators and officials, bombarded with questions, accused, criticized, his life and his character described, analysed, explained and defined by hostile agents whom he hardly knows, the moment and manner of his death decided upon in a seemingly arbitrary fashion by the powers that be, whoever they are, 'au nom du peuple français', Meursault is surely then—and the experience is not an uncommon one—*étourdi*. The word is his own:

> J'étais un peu étourdi aussi par tout ce monde dans cette salle close. J'ai regardé encore le prétoire et je n'ai distingué aucun visage. Je crois bien que d'abord je

ne m'étais pas rendu compte que tout le monde se pressait pour me voir.
D'habitude les gens ne s'occupaient pas de ma personne. Il m'a fallu un effort
pour comprendre que j'étais la cause de toute cette agitation.   (II.III, 131)

He is confused, estranged, disoriented; he feels that he does not belong,
that the events unfolding have nothing to do with him. It is little wonder
that during the cross-questioning he is not at his most articulate.

Now Meursault's behaviour during the cross-examining, and the terms
in which its description are couched, are deliberately ambiguous. Is he
unwilling or unable to answer satisfactorily the questions put to him?
Unwilling he may be, and we discuss the implications of this reading at a
later stage, but for the moment we suggest that much points to the fact
that he is unable to do so. He has not time to gather his thoughts, is in no
state to describe and justify his life: this latter, factitiously and
prejudicially, is all too glibly done for him. But as the trial proceeds the
beginnings of a desire to take part in the proceedings, to have his say,
takes hold of him. His tone changes from bewilderment to ironic
irritation:

> Une chose pourtant me gênait vaguement. Malgré mes préoccupations j'étais
> parfois tenté d'intervenir et mon avocat me disait alors: 'Taisez-vous, cela vaut
> mieux pour votre affaire'. En quelque sorte, on avait l'air de traiter cette affaire
> en dehors de moi. Tout se déroulait sans mon intervention. Mon sort se réglait
> sans qu'on prenne mon avis. De temps en temps, j'avais envie d'interrompre
> tout le monde et de dire: 'Mais tout de même, qui est l'accusé? C'est important
> d'être l'accusé. Et j'ai quelque chose à dire'. Mais toute réflexion faite, je n'avais
> rien à dire.   (II.IV, 153–4)

In the midst of this confusion he both wants to speak yet has nothing to
say, for he cannot find the words. It seems reasonable to suppose that back
in the cool and quiet of his cell, after the shock of the verdict, having
listened to an account of his life which bears little relation to the reality of
his lived experience, that he feels able to give his own account of things as
they happened. His *récit* is at one and the same time his 'counsel for the
defence', an exercise in self-exploration and self-justification, and the
giving of a shape and order to the confused, fragmented, chaotic data of
immediate experience.

Might it then be suggested that Meursault composes the *récit* (Part I and
Chapters I–IV of Part II) in between the moment of his condemnation,
which occurs at the end of Chapter IV, and the events described in the last
chapter? For in Chapter V of Part II the present or near-present in time
seems to catch up with the composing of the narrative.

Much of this chapter—the encounter with the *aumônier*, the closing passage, above all the opening section—recaptures the tone of immediacy so characteristic of Part I. But now the immediacy seems of an even more compelling and convincing nature:

> Pour la troisième fois, j'ai refusé de recevoir l'aumônier. Je n'ai rien à lui dire, je n'ai pas envie de parler, je le verrai bien assez tôt. Ce qui m'intéresse en ce moment, c'est d'échapper à la mécanique, de savoir si l'inévitable peut avoir une issue. On m'a changé de cellule. De celle-ci, lorsque je suis allongé, je vois le ciel et je ne vois que lui. Toutes mes journées se passent à regarder sur son visage le déclin des couleurs qui conduit le jour à la nuit. Couché, je passe les mains sous ma tête et j'attends.   (II.V, 167)

The narrative then moves into the past tense—a fusion of perfects and imperfects—where it remains until the end of the chapter. But this chapter opening—gentle, at times lyrical, always moving—conveys through its use of the present tense and its creation of an atmosphere of continuity in the present, a sense of immediacy of an order quite different from that found anywhere else in the *récit*. Meursault has lived through his crises; now we are living through the consequences with him.

So within the structure of the *récit* as we have it, within its chronological development, the portrait of Meursault presented is a dynamic one. Generally speaking he is seen to move from the world of experience to the world of reflection; from a state of unawareness based upon the unthinking, instinctive and spontaneous indulgence in the immediacy of experience, to a state of full awareness based upon the contemplation and written recreation of that same experience. The critical experiences which befall Meursault precipitate a 'fall into consciousness' and lead him to a profound understanding of his own situation and that of all mankind. Hence Camus's exploitation of the two Meursaults, aware and unaware, as a means of achieving his dual intentions: to give to the *récit* a structure and a narrative style allowing for both the impression of life lived in the present and the imposition of a considered, ordered recreation of it. 'La vie est sans style. Elle n'est qu'un mouvement qui court après sa forme sans la trouver jamais' (*HR*, 'Roman et révolte', 665). Art gives to life that style and form it seeks. Herein lies the brilliance and originality of Camus's narrative technique; he accords to Meursault, his character-narrator, the creative privilege of the artist. And Meursault is an artist, for taking the raw material of his *expérience vécue* he restructures and recomposes it in the *récit* in a way which gives it style, form and meaning. Here perhaps, and not in any biographical or other points of similarity, Camus may be identified with Meursault. Camus's technique in *L'Etranger* is born of and perfectly suited to his philosophical and aesthetic preoccupations at the time of writing it.

2

'L'Etranger' est une œuvre classique, une œuvre d'ordre, composée à propos de l'absurde et contre l'absurde. Sartre

Neither Camus's philosophical essay *Le Mythe de Sisyphe* (1942), nor *L'Envers et l'endroit* (1937), nor *Noces* (1939), taken singly or combined, 'explain' *L'Etranger*. Only the particular form and content of the work itself can hold the key to the *récit*. But Camus's theory of the Absurd, expounded and illustrated in various ways in these three collections of *essais*, informs *L'Etranger* in an essential manner.

There is nothing philosophically original, profound or for that matter complicated in the view of human existence contained in the Absurd. Eloquence, passion and emotional conviction, and not any particular intellectual sophistication, are the hallmarks of Camus's so-called philosophical essays. The topics dealt with and the opinions expressed therein are as old as thinking man: the existence or non-existence of God, the question of finite human existence and the notion of eternity, the relationship between the human world and the natural world, a contemplation of death and the manner in which such a contemplation makes us view the value and texture of our lives, the significance or insignificance of our human existence, these are Camus's basic preoccupations. On one level nothing could be more banal, on another nothing could be more universally or individually important; they are the things that matter. The stand that Camus takes on each of these issues, whilst not original, bites deep into us and forces us to examine the nature of our experience and our reactions to it.

At the root of the Absurd lies the atheistic postulate, the conviction that God does not exist, that the world and our presence in it are not part of a divine plan of eternal dimensions but are the result of chance, of a series of haphazard and gratuitous contingencies and coincidences:

Un monde qu'on peut expliquer même avec de mauvaises raisons est un monde familier. Mais au contraire dans un univers soudain privé d'illusions et de lumières l'homme se sent un étranger. Cet exil est sans recours puisqu'il est privé des souvenirs d'une patrie perdue ou de l'espoir d'une terre promise. (*MS*, 101)

Neither Eden nor Paradise exists; outside the confines of our existence on this earth we have come from nowhere, we are going nowhere. In this matter Meursault makes his position abundantly clear. In his encounters with the *juge d'instruction* (II.I) and with the *aumônier* (II.V) Meursault attests that the brand of Christianity each of them tries to impose upon him is of no interest to him. His attitude is based not upon a positive assertion of what he does believe and understand but upon a refutation of what he does not believe:

> Pourtant, aucune de ses certitudes ne valait un cheveu de femme. Il n'était même pas sûr d'être en vie puisqu'il vivait comme un mort. Moi, j'avais l'air d'avoir les mains vides. Mais j'étais sûr de moi, sûr de tout, plus sûr que lui, sûr de ma vie et de cette mort qui allait venir. Oui, je n'avais que cela. Mais, du moins je tenais cette vérité autant qu'elle me tenait. J'avais eu raison, j'avais encore raison, j'avais toujours raison. J'avais vécu de telle façon et j'aurais pu vivre de telle autre. J'avais fait ceci et je n'avais pas fait cela. Je n'avais pas fait telle chose alors que j'avais fait cette autre. Et après? C'était comme si j'avais attendu pendant tout le temps cette minute et cette petite aube où je serais justifié. Rien, rien n'avait d'importance et je savais bien pourquoi. (II.V, 185)

This rhetorical outburst—uncharacteristic of Meursault and all the more significant for being so—springs initially from his rage at the *aumônier's* attempts to convince him of the truth of Christianity, to persuade him to evaluate his life and imminent death within the framework of the Christian view of the human condition. In this respect Camus uses Meursault's angry tirade to launch a specific attack upon the Christian ethos. This in itself is important, for Christianity is in *L'Etranger*, as it is in so much of the rest of Camus's work, the particular philosophical system under attack. The notions of a divine creator, of man's guilt and his need for repentance, forgiveness and redemption, of the existence of an immortal soul, of the promise of eternal life in Paradise which will follow the brief interlude of his span of earthly existence, are all vigorously rejected by Meursault and his creator.

But the implications are wider. Christianity is by no means the only philosophical or religious system which claims to explain human existence in terms of reference which go beyond those provided by the data of our immediate earthly experience. It is not the only system claiming to perceive in life an order, logic and meaning, an overall significance within which individual experience may be codified and defined.

Meursault will accept no 'truth', no meaning beyond the fact of his intensely individual experience. It is its own truth, the absolute truth, relating to no other truth of a general order:

> Je peux tout réfuter dans ce monde qui m'entoure, me heurte ou me transporte, sauf ce chaos, ce hasard roi et cette divine équivalence qui naît de l'anarchie. Je ne sais pas si ce monde a un sens qui le dépasse. Mais je sais que je ne connais pas ce sens et qu'il m'est impossible pour le moment de la connaître. (*MS*, 136):

This assertion corresponds exactly to Meursault's position.

Death ends everything. Inherent in the Absurdist view of the world we find this conviction, closely related to the atheistic postulate, that man is finite, that in absolute terms his birth, life and death are the beginning, the middle and the end of all existence; where the individual experience is concerned the rest is nothingness. Such a postulate is, of course, directly opposed to the 'religious' belief—Christian and others—that death is a beginning, the threshold we cross in order to penetrate the barrier between ourselves and a new, and higher order of experience, that of life eternal whatever form it may take. In this respect, in terms of abstract logic at least, the Christian, for example, ought to welcome death with positive cheerfulness; but emotionally, it seems rarely to be the case, and few Christians want to die, or view the prospect with anything other than fear, apprehension, even horror. For we fear the unknown and death is, by definition, unknown and unknowable to us within our lived experience. In any case we do not wish to know it, shun the very thought of it, are as unwilling as we are incapable of grasping its ultimate reality, of really believing in it:

> on ne s'étonnera cependant jamais de ce que tout le monde vive comme si personne 'ne savait'. C'est qu'en réalité il n'y a pas d'expérience de la mort. Au sens propre n'est expérimenté que ce qui a été vécu et rendu conscient. Ici c'est tout juste s'il est possible de parler de la mort des autres. C'est un succédané, une vue de l'esprit et nous n'en sommes jamais très convaincus. (*MS*, 108).

Superficially we know that nothing is more certain than that we, our loved ones, all mankind must die. We assume, on this level, a resigned and stoical attitude. But insofar as we are prepared to experience imaginatively—and the experience must remain an imperfect though overwhelming one—the brutal, inescapable reality of our own elimination from the world, our attitude tends to be one of appalled and outraged disbelief. We recall Meursault's state of mind as his consciousness oscillates between these different levels of perception. (II.V, 175–6).

Reason predominates, perhaps in Meursault's case it ultimately prevails, but it cannot fully eliminate the irrational element surging into his consciousness. We have noted the structural and thematic importance of death in *L'Etranger*. Throughout the *récit*—from the death of his mother, the first death to impinge in any real way upon his consciousness ('c'est tout juste s'il est possible de parler de la mort des autres'), through his involvement in the violent death of the Arab, to his eventual facing of imminent execution—Meursault moves gradually from the innocence of living 'comme si personne ne savait' to a lucid awareness and imaginatively powerful experience of the reality of his own death. In describing this growth in awareness Meursault, the retrospective narrator, explores the tension arising within himself as a result of the confrontation of these two contrasting levels of consciousness, the lucid Meursault recalls a former self who lived happily in a 'paradise' he now knows never really existed.

The 'fall into consciousness', which plays such a vital role in Camus's fictional work—witness not only Meursault in *L'Etranger*, but also the citizens of Oran in *La Peste*, Jean-Baptiste Clamence in *La Chute*—and accords it a certain tragic dimension, is an essential feature of man's experience and knowledge of the Absurd: 'Nous prenons l'habitude de vivre avant d'acquérir celle de penser' (*MS*, 102). . . . 'Commencer à penser, c'est commencer d'être miné' (*MS*, 100). This is the crux of the matter. To a considerable degree, man's peace of mind may be preserved, many of his inner tensions avoided as long as he can continue to live in a state of unawareness of the nature of the world and his position in it. In this respect habit, routine, the mechanical response to a mechanical existence may be seen as subconsciously employed weapons of self-defence against the incursion of the absurd into the consciousness:

> Lever, tramway, quatre heures de bureau, ou d'usine, repas, tramway, quatre heures de travail, repas, sommeil et lundi mardi mercredi jeudi vendredi et samedi sur le même rythme, cette route se suit aisément la plupart du temps. Un jour seulement, le 'pourquoi' s'élève et tout commence dans cette lassitude teintée d'étonnement. (*MS*, 107)

Once the question has been asked the process begins whereby the illusory notion of a life based on order, harmony, reason and meaningfulness is replaced by the knowledge that life is absurd. The Absurd is disparity: the disparity between man's desire for unity and the inescapable fact of the dualism of his nature; the disparity between his impulse to be completely at one with the world of nature and the world of human society and the fact of his inability to do so; the disparity between his aspiration to eternal life and the fact of his finite, mortal being; the disparity between his attempt to give his life a meaning and the fact of the futility and emptiness of his efforts. Death, chance, the irrationality and unintelligibility of the world impose themselves upon him and destroy his every ambition. Thus man as he is is irreconcilable with the world in which he lives. Therein lies the Absurd. It is essentially then a disparity, a *divorce*:

> 'L'absurde est essentiellement un divorce. Il n'est ni dans l'un ni dans l'autre des éléments comparés. Il naît de leur confrontation. Sur le plan de l'intelligence je peux dire que l'absurde n'est pas dans l'homme (si une pareille métaphore pourrait avoir un sens), ni dans le monde, mais dans leur présence commune. (*MS*, 120)

Most importantly, a belief in the absurd nature of the human condition does not eliminate from the mind the powerful presence of a sharply contrasting response to the world of experience. And this, for Camus, is vital: 'Cette nostalgie d'unité, cet appétit d'absolu illustre le mouvement essentiel du drame humain' (*MS*, 110). He does of course refute such tendencies, for they are examples of the human spirit's inability to accept the unpalatable fact of absurd reality, seeking to cull from existence a meaning based on an illusion. But they are strong tendencies within his own temperament and, as such, play a part in *L'Etranger*, wherein a conflict exists in Meursault between the promptings of emotion, instinct and imagination and the dictates of reason, reflection and intelligence. Here is the paradox; despite the cruel truth of the Absurd there are in human experience moments when a sense of harmony, of the beauty of life, of union and communion prevails. Much of *Noces* is a lyrical celebration of this fact:

> Mer, campagne, silence, parfums de cette terre, je m'emplissais d'une vie odorante et je mordais dans le fruit déjà doré du monde, bouleversé de sentir son jus sucré et fort couler le long de mes lèvres. Non, ce n'était pas moi qui comptais, ni le monde, mais seulement l'accord et le silence qui de lui à moi faisait naître l'amour. Amour que je n'avais pas la faiblesse de revendiquer pour moi seul, conscient et orgueilleux de le partager avec toute une race née du

soleil et de la mer, vivante et savoureuse, qui puise sa grandeur dans sa simplicité et, debout sur les plages, adresse son sourire complice au sourire éclatant de ses ciels. (*Noces à Tipasa*, 60)

Moments such as this, conveying powerfully the notion of an idyllic communion between man and nature, between man and man, the edenic quality of existence, the sense of the beauty and oneness of all reaction, intoxicate the experiencer and invite him to believe in a benevolent universe, in a world of harmony and order with which he is at one. Meursault is no stranger to such experience; it is in his nature to seek it, and enjoy it. And such in large measure, we infer from Part I, is his experience of life until the moment of the 'fall into consciousness', the dawning of his awareness of the reality of his position in the world. It occurs immediately after the murder:

. . . et c'est là . . . que tout a commencé. . . . J'ai compris que j'avais détruit l'équilibre du jour, le silence exceptionnel d'une plage où j'avais été heureux. (I.IV, 95)

The language here assumes an added, figurative dimension. For it is not just the harmony of that particular day, the unusual silence of that particular beach which are referred to. Contained within these words is the recognition of the loss of an edenic existence, the shattering of an illusion. Harmony, peace and unity have gone; they are replaced by disruption and divorce. The reality of his condition, the absurd, penetrates Meursault's consciousness for the first time. Once there, it never leaves him and Meursault, the retrospective narrator, informs his self-portrait in Part I with a significance of which his former self, until this crucial moment, remained completely unaware.

The natural elements are like Janus; they are double-faced. The givers of life, they seem to offer at times the image of a creation based on order, harmony and eternity in which man shares. But for Camus they also reflect cruelly the true nature of our human condition and destiny, where intimations of unity and eternity are snatched from us to be replaced by the ultimate realities of suffering and death. Thus the mood of *Noces* is confronted and finally defeated by the dominant mood of *L'Envers et l'endroit* and the basic philosophic postulate presented in *Le Mythe de Sisyphe*.

The tone of *L'Envers et L'endroit* is ironic, bitter, redolent of an attitude of cynicism, even cruelty, characteristics which do not quite conceal the overall sense of distress and disenchantment which emanate from the passage. The omnipresence of death, the loneliness and misery of old age, the unwitting cruelty and apparent insensitivity of the young, the inevitable descent into solitude, abandonment and final oblivion far outweigh in preponderance the sense of any joy to be gained from living. The mood is dark, sardonic, world-weary.

The major preoccupations of these essays are reflected in the content of Part I of *L'Etranger*. Between the incidence of the two deaths, which provide the structural and thematic framework within which the narrative takes shape, Meursault devotes a considerable amount of the *récit* to the atmosphere of the *asile*, to the behaviour, appearance and existence of the people found there; to the description of the relationship between the wretched Salamano and his scabby dog; to the personality of Raymond, violent, ugly, grotesque, and the account of his unsavoury rapport with his mistress. All of them are concerned with the ugly, violent, even repellent side of human experience, with brutality, loneliness, decrepitude and death. All are accorded a degree of attention within the narrative by Meursault which indicates that they exercise a particular fascination for him. Coming to combat the other side of nature and of human experience, closely related both in themselves and within the thematic structure of the book to the notion of death, they give to the fabric of the *récit* a texture into which is persistently interwoven Meursault's contemplation of the overriding facts of the human condition: a period of illusion followed inevitably by the experience of decay, abandonment, isolation and death. Part I contains a markedly morbid element.

And in Part II Meursault facing now the possibility of his own imminent death, and all that that implies, harks back longingly to the time of his 'freedom'; first in the specific, literal sense, to the freedom denied him by his physical imprisonment; secondly, in the symbolic sense, to the freedom, albeit illusory, of 'l'équilibre du jour, le silence exceptionnel d'une plage où j'avais été heureux.' His nostalgia for that time never leaves him:

La prison était tout en haut de la ville et, par une petite fenêtre, je pouvais voir la mer. C'est un jour que j'étais agrippé au barreaux, mon visage tendu vers la lumière, qu'un gardien est entré et m'a dit que j'avais une visite. (II.II, 114)

a marvellous moment in the narrative where the language, simple, concrete, immediate, assumes symbolic dimensions. But his return to freedom on a psychological and symbolic level, unlike his possible return to freedom in a legal and physical sense, is already impossible. His loss of physical freedom and imprisonment are images of the ultimate reality of his human condition. His consciousness can never again divest itself of this.

For Camus the recognition of the absurdity of existence is a profoundly emotional experience, the most overwhelming of all:

> A partir du moment où elle est reconnue, l'absurdité est une passion, la plus déchirante de toutes. Mais savoir si l'on peut vivre avec ses passions, savoir si l'on peut accepter leur loi profonde qui est de brûler le coeur que dans le même temps elles exaltent, voilà toute la question. (*MS*, 113)

In *L'Etranger* the solution which both author and character find to the problem of living with this passion is of an aesthetic order. Let us return to the reference to Gide quoted earlier:

> Connaissant bien l'anarchie de ma nature, j'ai besoin de me donner en art des barrières. Gide m'a appris à le faire. Sa conception du classicisme considéré comme un romantisme dompté est la mienne.

Few would dispute that the Absurd, as a philosophical notion and as a literary phenomenon, has its roots in the Romantic movement. Camus's literary art consists in the manner to which he subjects the passion, the anarchic impulse, the emotional *élan* of his nature to the severe discipline of expression imposed by the classical canon. This aesthetic process is of great psychological and philosophical importance.

3

In 1943, the year following the publication of *L'Etranger*, appeared *L'Intelligence et l'échafaud*, Camus's essay on the French *esprit classique* referring particularly to the art of the novel and more particularly to Madame de Lafayette's *La Princesse de Clèves*. In this short and perceptive essay Camus is as much concerned to explore his own artistic procedure as he is to express his admiration of writers working within what he considers to be the classical tradition. To his knowledge of the aesthetic demands of the classical canon—clarity, simplicity, order and measure of expression—he brings the insight of an artist aware of matters of a psychological and philosophical order fundamentally inseparable from this aesthetic doctrine.

This discipline of expression which the classical author imposes upon himself has a specific intention which goes well beyond the bounds of an *exercice de style*:

> Et cette recherche d'un langage intelligible qui doit recouvrir la démesure de son destin, le conduit à dire non pas ce qui lui plaît mais seulement ce qu'il faut. Une grande partie du génie romanesque français tient dans cet effort éclairé pour donner aux cris de passion l'ordre d'un langage pur. (*IE*, 1897)

The control exercised in classical style is representative of an ordering and controlling, by character and author, of the very substance of an appalling destiny, of the initially passionate emotional explosion which accompanies its recognition. Concentration upon the essential of the matter, the adoption of a pure and lucid means of expressing it, are the means whereby author and character give measure to the *démesure du destin*. We are led to think of the lucidity, the control and the measure of expression with which Camus and his character-narrator describe for us the destiny confronting the man who recognizes the Absurd, that 'passion, la plus déchirante de toutes'.

Thus in speaking of the art of Madame de Lafayette, and in illustrating the tragic situation of her characters and their reaction to this situation, Camus propounds the following:

> Mais il est bien évident que cet art naît d'une infinie possibilité de souffrance et d'une décision arrêtée de s'en rendre maître par le discours. Rien ne dit mieux cette détresse disciplinée, cette lumière puissante dont l'intelligence transfigure la douleur qu'une admirable phrase de *La Princesse de Clèves*: 'Je lui dit que tant que son affliction avait eu des bornes, je l'avais approuvée et que j'y étais entrée; mais que je ne le plaindrais plus s'il s'abandonnait au désespoir et s'il perdait la raison'. Ce ton est magnifique. Il postule qu'une certaine force de l'âme peut poser des bornes au malheur en censurant son expression. Il fait entrer l'art dans la vie en donnant à l'homme en lutte contre son destin les forces du langage. (*IE*, 1900)

From *La Princesse de Clèves* to *L'Etranger* we move from French aristocratic life to the life of a French Algerian clerk, from the dignity of the courtly setting to the humdrum, sometimes unsavoury atmosphere of Meursault's life in Algiers, from the threat of destruction by *l'amour-passion* to the threat of engulfment by an awareness of the Absurd. The areas, the atmosphere, the values differ greatly in the two books. But the artistic premises of each author, the reactions of each character to a crisis in their experience are fundamentally the same. The crisis, the tragedy is to be dominated, triumphed over. And the self-discipline, the strength of mind needed to achieve this triumph to avoid despair and loss of reason, to limit the extent and the impact of misfortune, are achieved by a conscious manipulation of the language used by the protagonist first to conceive of his situation and then to give expression to it.

Concealing an infinite source of possible suffering, the classical style—sober, measured, lucid, controlled—is, for both author and character, the principal defence against the prospect of a destiny which threatens to engulf them, as it is the instrument whereby they are able to transcend the incidence of that destiny. Where Meursault, no less than where Madame de Clèves is concerned, there is no lack of sensitivity, no lack of passion. There is rather, in the pursuit of human dignity and spiritual survival, a refusal to indulge in their unbridled expression.

Intelligence, reason and discipline of expression come to impose themselves upon 'l'anarchie de ma nature': '[L'intelligence] n'apporte pas seulement sa conception, elle est en même temps un principe d'une merveilleuse économie et d'une sorte de monotonie passionnée. Elle est à la fois créatrice et mécanicienne' (*IE*, 1898). There can be no better summary than this of the art of the *récit* in *L'Etranger* in which Camus and Meursault are, artistically, at one 'pour donner aux cris de passion l'ordre d'un langage pur'.

3. Character and Consequence

L'Etranger

Qui aimes-tu le mieux, homme énigmatique, dis? ton père, ta mère, ta soeur ou ton frère?

Je n'ai ni père, ni mère, ni soeur, ni frère.

Tes amis?

Vous vous servez là d'une parole dont le sens m'est resté jusqu'à ce jour inconnu.

Ta patrie?

J'ignore sous quelle latitude elle est située.

La beauté?

Je l'aimerais volontiers, déesse et immortelle.

L'or?

Je le hais comme vous haïssez Dieu.

Et qu'aimes-tu donc, extraordinaire étranger?
J'aime les nuages . . . les nuages qui passent . . . là-bas . . . là-bas . . . les
merveilleux nuages. (Baudelaire, *Le Spleen de Paris*)

Overtly at least, Part I is not, on the part of either Camus or Meursault, an exercise in the revelation of character. Yet in exploring certain structural features of the narrative we may gain some understanding of Meursault's character and the bearing it has upon his destiny. Camus creates a character who, in responding instinctively to the world of the Absurd, shapes his destiny.

On the face of it the Meursault of Part I is a well-liked, easy-going character; Marie, Céleste, Emmanuel, Masson, Raymond, Salamano, all like him; until it comes to the trial the director and the caretaker of the *asile* seem to have nothing against him. His *patron* is, of course, disappointed that he refuses promotion. In general, however, they seem to get on reasonably and Meursault works quite well in his modest employment. His lack of ambition indicates, in fact, that he is well satisfied with the environment and conditions in which he lives. He is an accommodating and understanding person: he understands that his *patron* should feel annoyed that his journey to the funeral means that he gets four consecutive days off work, is sorry to disappoint him by not taking the job in Paris and appreciates his feelings in the matter; he seems quite prepared to marry Marie if that is what she wants; he is, as both Raymond and Salamano know, a very good and sympathetic listener. He respects the behaviour and opinions of other people to an unusual degree; his reaction to Salamano and, more disturbingly, to Raymond are clear indication of this. He also respects other people's privacy as, reasonably enough, he likes his own to be respected ('Je ne voulais pas déjeuner chez Céleste comme d'habitude parce que, certainement, ils m'auraient posé des questions et je n'aime pas cela' (I.II, 36)). He lives as he pleases but in a way which causes the minimum possible annoyance or disturbance to other people. He is then, tolerant, satisfied with his lot, friendly, ready to listen but never prying; what more can one ask?

Meursault seems to be 'free', but it is a form of freedom which the existentialist would describe, rightly or wrongly, as a factitious freedom. For the existentialist, authentic freedom is achieved through commitment; commitment to a political or religious ideal, to a person or group of people, to a cause. Paradoxically perhaps, authentic existentialist freedom is achieved through a giving of the self. But Meursault, on the

contrary, seems totally uncommitted. He has no religious or political
beliefs, indeed seems to have no view of life at all, does his job but is not
devoted to his career, and seems to be quite devoid of any positive moral
or ethical viewpoint. His freedom is the freedom of non-involvement, of
non-commitment; it is negative in nature and this is reflected in his
relationship with others. Socially, morally, emotionally, it is part of
Meursault's make-up to keep other people at arm's length. This does not
appear to be the result of a conscious decision or policy but rather a fact of
his nature; he agrees, in somewhat lukewarm fashion, to marry Marie but
is in no way emotionally involved with her; his mother, whom he loves
'comme tout le monde' he puts in an old people's home because it seemed
the best and most natural thing to do in the circumstances; his attitude to
Raymond—whose behaviour surely cries out for condemnation on the
part of any morally concerned person—is totally devoid of moral
judgment, or of any judgment at all, for or against; his murdering of the
Arab—and this remains true throughout Part II—causes him no moral
concern. Where *people* are concerned Meursault is unemotional,
unconcerned, amoral. He is fundamentally an egotist. There is nothing
'wrong' in that. It is certainly no crime.

His response to nature is far more positive. It is when his senses are
invaded by the heat and light of the sun, the softness and coolness of the
sea, the smell of the night, of flowers, of the earth, that he is most intensely
alive. He instinctively closes himself to humanity and opens himself to the
natural world. It is when we look at these general features of Meursault's
character operating simultaneously within the detailed structures of the
narrative that a tight-knit pattern emerges.

In Chapter I the following detailed incidents occur:

> J'ai couru pour ne pas manquer le départ. Cette hâte, cette course, c'est à cause
> de tout cela sans doute, ajouté aux cahots, à l'odeur d'essence, à la réverbération
> de la route et du ciel que je me suis assoupi. J'ai dormi pendant presque tout le
> trajet. Et quand je me suis réveillé j'étais tassé contre un militaire qui m'a souri
> et qui m'a demandé si je venais de loin. J'ai dit 'oui' pour n'avoir plus à
> parler. (I.I, 10–11)

Then:

> Quand elle est partie, le concierge a parlé: 'Je vais vous laisser seul.' Je ne sais
> pas quel geste j'ai fait, mais il est resté, debout derrière moi. Cette présence dans
> mon dos me gênait. La pièce était pleine d'une belle lumière de fin d'après-midi.
> Deux frelons bourdonnaient contre la verrière. Et je sentais le sommeil me
> gagner. (15)

Then:

> La garde était aussi au fond, le dos tourné. Je ne voyais pas ce qu'elle faisait. Mais au mouvement de ses bras je pouvais croire qu'elle tricotait. Il faisait doux, le café m'avait réchauffé et par la porte ouverte entrait une odeur de nuit et de fleurs. Je crois que j'ai somnolé un peu.   (I.I, 18)

The chapter concludes:

> J'ai encore gardé quelques images de cette journée: par exemple le visage de Pérez quand, pour la dernière fois, il nous a rejoints près du village. De grosses larmes d'énervement et de peine ruisselaient sur ses joues. Mais, à cause des rides, elles ne s'écoulaient pas. Elles s'étalaient, se rejoignaient et formaient un vernis d'eau sur ce visage détruit. Il y a eu encore l'église et les villageois sur les trottoirs, les géraniums rouges sur les tombes du cimetière, l'évanouissement de Pérez (on eût dit un pantin disloqué), la terre couleur de sang qui roulait sur la bière de maman, la chair blanche des racines qui s'y mêlaient, encore du monde, des voix, le village, l'attente devant un café, l'incessant ronflement du moteur, et ma joie quand l'autobus est entré dans le nid de lumière d'Alger et que j'ai pensé que j'allais me coucher pendant douze heures.   (I.I, 30–31)

Taken by themselves, the first three of these four passages are not particularly remarkable in any way. The sentences are short and written in simple, direct, non-figurative language. In content they seem typical of the uneventful and insignificant events which, falling naturally into the account of the detail of Meursault's day-to-day experience, make up a considerable proportion of Part I. But taken together they assume a degree of significance, for a quite striking structural pattern emerges. In each of these three passages four elements are present: Meursault, another human being, an effect upon the senses by the surrounding (predominantly natural) world, and sleep. Meursault's reactions to these three events are clear enough. In two of the three passages he is plainly and explicitly irritated by the other human presence, in the third we may infer a certain degree of distaste. In the second and third passage he turns away from the human presence, opens himself to sensory experience and loses himself in sleep; in the first passage the order of events is reversed, but exactly the same processes occur and the overall effect is the same.

To these four elements present in the text we may add a fifth, present in Meursault's mind, death; the first passage occurs during his journey to the *asile*, the other two during the vigil. All five elements come together in the fourth passage we have quoted, the culmination and climax of Chapter I.

In this fourth passage the narrative style and perspective are in sharp contrast to those found in the preceding three, and indeed in the rest of the chapter. The length, the rhythm, the detailed accumulation of the *images de cette journée*, the impressionistic nature of the last sentence combine therein to create an atmosphere of tension, to convey the fevered, nightmarish quality of Meursault's state of mind induced by his experience. This tension is the result of the now profuse and confused juxtaposing of those same elements found within the structures of the three earlier passages. The human world: Pérez, voices, the village, the café; the natural world: the red geraniums on the graves, the blood-red earth, the white roots; death, now directly present in the narrative and, in the powerfully evocative *la terre couleur de sang qui roulait sur la bière de maman*, bringing to mind the ultimate end of human life within the natural order, all these elements fuse in Meursault's consciousness to create a tension from which he must escape. And once more he escapes, now thankfully, into the oblivion of sleep.

In none of these passages, taken individually, can we say that Meursault's 'dropping off', or his pleasurable anticipation of a good sleep, make any particular impact on the reader. Each of the moments at which he falls asleep, or looks forward to doing so, occurs in a perfectly natural and unremarkable manner, a manner reflecting the tendency of any normal human being, given the circumstances described. Such is the stamp of the narrative. But taken collectively, and in conjunction with certain critical moments found later in the *récit*, they assume a symbolic significance.

As Meursault walks, alone, along the beach towards the Arab, towards the event around which the whole book is to revolve, we learn:

> Je voyais de loin la petite masse sombre du rocher entourée d'un halo aveuglant par la lumière et la poussière de mer. Je pensais à la source fraîche derrière le rocher. J'avais envie de retrouver le murmure de son eau, envie de fuir le soleil, l'effort et les pleurs de femme, envie enfin de retrouver l'ombre et son repos. Mais quand j'ai été plus près, j'ai vu que le type de Raymond était revenu. (I.VI, 92)

The same four elements are present: Meursault, another human presence, the natural world, and, in *l'ombre et son repos* by extension, the desire to sleep. The fifth element, death, in this case the death of the Arab, is imminent. Again, the description of each of the elements contained within this structure has its roots in the immediacy of concrete experience. The early afternoon sun is unbearably hot and Meursault, quite naturally, wishes to shelter from it; walking along the beach in this heat entails a considerable *effort* on his part; the women's tears are the tears of Madam Masson and Marie, much upset by the sight of Raymond's knife wounds; Meursault is, understandably, put out to find that the Arab already occupies the cool and shady spot he seeks. Thus we may explain this short paragraph, but such an explanation has little bearing upon the effect produced in us by its rhythmic structure, its vocabulary, its powers of suggestiveness.

The rhythm and much of the vocabulary are evocative of the Bible—the water springing from the rock, men will toil and women will weep, the well-worn epithets of shade and rest symbolizing death as a release from the cares of this mortal coil—evocative of a view of the human condition in which death is seen as an event freeing man from the chains of his earthly experience. The narrative portrays, symbolically, a Meursault bent on shaking himself free of the toil and tearfulness of life and embracing the peace and rest to be found in death. A human presence, the symbol of earthly existence, stands in his way.

Let us turn to a further critical moment in the narrative, part of the concluding section, which occurs immediately after the departure of the violently abused *aumônier*:

> Lui parti, j'ai retrouvé le calme. J'étais épuisé et je me suis jeté sur ma couchette. Je crois que j'ai dormi parce que je me suis réveillé avec des étoiles sur le visage. Des bruits de campagne montaient jusqu'à moi. Des odeurs de nuit, de terre et de sel rafraîchissaient mes tempes. La merveilleuse paix de cet été endormi entrait en moi comme une marée. A ce moment, et à la limite de la nuit, des sirènes ont hurlé. Elles annonçaient des départs pour un monde qui maintenant m'étaient à jamais indifférent. . . . Comme si cette grande colère m'avait purgé du mal, vidé d'espoir, devant cette nuit chargé de signes et d'étoiles, je m'ouvrais pour la première fois à la tendre indifférence du monde. (II.V, 187–8)

Again the same basic elements are found within the structure of the crucial passage: Meursault, of course; the human world of the *aumônier*, the cause of his anger, now departed, and of the factory hooters calling men to life in a world which Meursault no longer cares about; the natural world evoked in controlledly lyrical terms and seen to be invading him in a manner which induces a sense of peace and resignation within him; sleep, the bridge between his rejection of the *aumônier* and all he stands for and his opening of himself, through sensory experience, to the embrace of the natural world. The fifth element, death, now Meursault's own imminent death, looms large in the narrative.

These sections of the narrative—the four passages from Chapter I, the paragraph from Chapter VI, the part of the concluding section of the final chapter—occur precisely at the beginning, the middle and the end of the book. Thus they relate intimately to what we have seen earlier to be the basic structural feature of L'Etranger; it begins with a death (Meursault's mother), it has as its central pivot a death (the Arab), it ends with a death (Meursault). And thus they relate no less intimately to the central thematic preoccupation of the book, Meursault's encounters with death and his eventually formed attitude towards it. In the manner of their telling they relate further to that equally important structural and thematic phenomenon, Meursault's development, as his story unfolds, from a state of unawareness to one of lucid awareness and acceptance. For when, in the final chapter, he states: 'Je m'ouvrais pour la première fois à la tendre indifférence du monde' (II.V, 188) this is at once true and not true. It is true in that he does so at this moment for the first time *in full consciousness* of what he is doing and of its implications; the Meursault of the final chapter is a fully aware individual. It is not true in that the earlier unaware Meursault behaves instinctively and spontaneously in exactly the same way. The final philosophical *prise de position* is the conscious rationalization and confirmation of an existence lived in an earlier state of unawareness. The specific destiny awaiting him is dictated by the impulses innate in his character.

In a social and historical context, it has been argued that the trial and condemnation to death of Meursault are improbable and unconvincing, that at that time in that place Meursault would not have been executed for the particular crime he committed. The argument carries some weight. But, for Camus, Meursault's death is a fictional necessity. The demands of factual probability are overridden by the author's philosophical intentions in L'Etranger and by the psychological impulses of his character-narrator which drive him to his death. These two concepts combine to give the *récit* its artistically necessary conclusion.

In the closing paragraphs of the work Meursault's reactions to the human world, the natural world and death are given clear expression by a now lucidly aware man resigned to his fate. The human world has rejected him, condemned him to be executed, so he in his turn rejects that world, opens himself to the natural world and accepts, even welcomes death.

But at this point in his life such a reaction is perhaps forced upon him. There seems now to be no alternative to execution and death: he therefore adopts the only attitude possible in the circumstances. The rejection of Meursault's appeal is a blow to him. There is no doubt that, on an important level of his being, Meursault wants to live, to pursue the life which he believes is all creation has to offer him. But there is some suggestion that, once the reality of death has entered his experience—and this occurs at the time of his mother's death—on another level of his being there exists a subconscious compulsion towards first a symbolic and then a literal enactment of his own death. On this matter we remain in the realm of speculation, but the indications are there. They present themselves when we take in conjunction with the closing paragraphs the sections of Part I mentioned above.

Examining the structural pattern we have seen to emerge in the first chapter, we note Meursault's instinctive tendency to turn away from the human world, to lose the self and the consciousness in the oblivion of a sleep brought about largely through the invasion of his senses by the natural world. This is not an unusual phenomenon and each of the incidents referred to occurs convincingly at the level of normal, concrete experience. But the reiterative nature of the structure of these passages may be seen to contain a symbolic significance, particularly when we relate them to the moment in Chapter VI referred to, where not only does the same structural phenomenon occur, but where the specific language used is clearly symbolic in nature. The powerfully evocative quality of this language—'J'avais envie de retrouver le murmure de son eau, envie de fuir le soleil et les pleurs de femme, envie enfin de retrouver l'ombre et son repos'—suggests that Meursault seeks in nature not only the oblivion of sleep but also the final oblivion of death. Nature and death, Meursault's opening of the self to nature and his subconscious impulse to embrace death, are indivisibly present in the text. Herein we find the essential ambiguity of his character; the simultaneous presence within him of the desire to live as intensely as possible in the immediacy of the present and of the impulse to experience the ultimate finality of death. The natural world is the arena of these conflicting tendencies of his character and it is well-suited to accommodate them. For the features of the absurd natural world are the features of Janus.

Death is present in the narrative on the two crucial occasions in Part I when nature, the giver of life, the creator of a sense of the harmony and oneness of human experience, reveals its other face:

J'étais surpris de la rapidité avec laquelle le soleil montait dans le ciel. Je me suis aperçu qu'il y avait déjà longtemps que la campagne bourdonnait du chant des insectes et de crépitements d'herbe. La sueur coulait sur mes joues. Comme je n'avais pas de chapeau, je m'éventais avec mon mouchoir. . . . Il me semblait que le convoi marchait un peu vite. Autour de moi, c'était toujours la même campagne lumineuse gorgée de soleil. L'éclat du ciel était insoutenable. . . . J'étais un peu perdu entre le ciel bleu et blanc et la monotonie de ces couleurs, noir gluant du goudron ouvert, noir terne des habits, noir laqué de la voiture. Tout cela, le soleil, l'odeur de cuir et de crottin de la voiture, celle du vernis et celle de l'encens, la fatigue d'une nuit d'insomnie, me troublait le regard et les idées. . . . Tout s'est passé ensuite avec tant de précipitation, de certitude et de naturel, que je ne me souviens plus de rien. (I.I, 28–30)

Because of the vigil Meursault has not slept the previous night. As he follows the funeral procession death is omnipresent in his mind; his mother's body lies in the coffin, her death and death in general are reflected figuratively in the black of the tar, the mourners' clothing, the funeral carriage. In the presence of death Meursault is uncomfortable and disorientated, a state of mind and body apparently brought about by the unbearable heat of the sun.

The effect produced by the presence of death in his mind and the simultaneous invasion of his senses by the hostile forces of nature is taken up again, in a greatly intensified manner, at a later point in the narrative:

C'était le même éclatement rouge. Sur le sable, la mer haletait de toute la respiration rapide et étouffée de ses petites vagues. Je marchais lentement vers les rochers et je sentais mon front se gonfler sous le soleil. Toute cette chaleur s'appuyait sur moi et s'opposait à mon avance. Et chaque fois que je sentais son grand souffle chaud sur mon visage, je serrais les dents, je fermais les poings dans les poches de mon pantalon, je me tendais tout entier pour triompher du soleil et de cette ivresse opaque qu'il me déversait. . . . C'était le même soleil, la même lumière sur le même sable qui se prolongeait ici. . . . C'était le même soleil que le jour où j'avais enterré maman et, comme alors, le front surtout me faisait mal et toutes ses veines battaient ensemble sous la peau. . . . Je ne sentais plus que les cymbales du soleil sur mon front et, indistinctement, le glaive éclatant jailli du couteau toujours en face de moi. Cette épée brûlante rongeait mes cils et fouillait mes yeux douloureux. C'est alors que tout a vacillé. La mer a charrié un souffle épais et ardent. Il m'a semblé que le ciel s'ouvrait sur toute son étendue pour laisser pleuvoir du feu. Tout mon être s'est tendu et j'ai crispé ma main sur le revolver. (I.VI, 91–5)

Meursault then kills the Arab. In the detail of his account of his walk along the beach he recalls in specific terms that other occasion when, in the presence of death, the natural elements came to produce a similar effect in him. He is disorientated, overwhelmed, hypnotized. Whatever the circumstances, Meursault is always susceptible to the natural world, particularly responsive to its promptings. Now, as the tone of the narrative heightens to produce a nightmarish, almost hallucinatory effect, that natural world, in hostile and destructive mood, seems to take possession of him, to make of him its puppet, its instrument of death. The style of the narrative, usually so flat, so controlled, measured and non-figurative, is now one in which the rhythmic structure of the sentences, singly and combined, and the accumulation of images, similes and metaphors, combine to create an atmosphere of unbearable tension, one where Meursault seems to lose all control of his actions, all grasp of reality. The natural elements, personified or near personified, assume the role of an active and malevolent force of destiny bent on the destruction of their human plaything.

To a considerable degree the style and tone of the narrative invite us to consider the murder of the Arab as the result of the invasion and possession of Meursault, the helpless human victim, by external, hostile elemental forces whose will he is powerless to oppose. The natural elements may then be seen as a modern equivalent of the Furies. Certainly the text offers the possibility of such an interpretation. It is an attractive one for it implies the absence on Meursault's part of any responsibility whatsoever for the murder. But the relationship between Meursault, violence and nature, is of a more complex order.

On the Sunday of the murder Meursault awakes out of sorts:

Le dimanche j'ai eu de la peine à me réveiller et il a fallu que Marie m'appelle et me secoue. Nous n'avons pas mangé parce que nous voulions nous baigner tôt. Je me sentais tout à fait vide et j'avais un peu mal à la tête. Ma cigarette avait un goût amer. Marie s'est moquée de moi parce qu'elle disait que j'avais 'une tête d'enterrement'. . . . Dans la rue, à cause de ma fatigue et aussi parce que nous n'avions pas ouvert les persiennes, le jour, déjà plein de soleil, m'a frappé comme une gifle. (I.VI, 77)

We note in the closing words of the passage, that Meursault, in referring to the effect of the sun upon him, uses an image of physical violence. This is not surprising. Our reaction to the heat and light of the sun—or to almost any natural phenomenon—is largely subjective. If we feel well the morning sun cheers us; if we have a headache it weighs upon us, seems to assault us. Meursault is no exception. By half-past eleven that morning

Meursault, having enjoyed a swim, has eaten a large meal, drunk a great
deal of wine and smoked heavily. He is still feeling out of sorts (I.VI, 84).
He then proceeds to walk along the beach three times in the heat of the
midday sun, and from the moment the first walk begins the natural
elements are described in terms similar to those we have witnessed in the
moments immediately preceding the murder (I.VI, 85).

Camus again uses the chapter opening to establish a framework,
temporal or thematic, for what is to follow. It is all too easy, given the
climactic build-up of subsequent events, and the imposing nature of their
description, to ignore or underestimate the importance of the opening
section of Chapter VI, couched as it is in relatively undramatic terms.
But, importantly, it presents in a quite different light the relationship
between Meursault's state of mind and his description of the natural
elements. For it suggests that the natural world is, as Meursault later
describes it, *indifférent*, and that his subjective response to this unchanging,
non-intentioned phenomenon is dictated by an existing physical and
mental condition. Further, he does, when brought back to his senses by
the first shot, assert his personal responsibility—and goes on to confirm
it:

> J'ai compris que j'avais détruit l'équilibre du jour, le silence exceptionnel d'une
> plage où j'avais été heureux. Alors j'ai tiré encore quatre fois sur un corps
> inerte . . . (I.VI, 95)

The variation in style is the vehicle for two sharply conflicting
philosophical principles which, taken together, create a sense of
ambiguity. And taken together they must be; for ambiguity, operating
within the movement of the narrative from the realistic to the symbolic,
the concrete to the poetic, is the hallmark of the *récit*. Where Meursault's
relationship with nature and the violence consequent upon it are
concerned, it is not ultimately a question of cause and effect, one way or
the other, but of fusion and interreaction: 'l'absurde n'est pas dans
l'homme ni dans le monde mais dans leur présence commune.' It is
Meursault's instinctive response to the inherently absurd relationship
between himself and the natural world, where death comes to deny the
human aspiration towards unity of existence and eternal life, which leads
him to murder. His instinctive response to the human world, that other
half of the absurd equation, plays no less a part.

Whilst we find in Meursault the constant tendency to close himself to
the human world and open himself to the natural world, certain aspects of

the human world do fascinate him. We noted earlier that in his account of his life from the time of his mother's death to the murder of the Arab, Meursault accords particular importance to his description of the lonely and decrepit inmates of the *asile*, pathetic and grotesque in the way they cling to life. He accords even greater importance to the equally lonely and grotesque Salamano, who re-enacts in somewhat gruesome manner, through his relationship with his dog, the habits and practices of his former marriage. Meursault is compulsively drawn to the more ugly and morbid elements in human experience. This may well not have been the case in his earlier life but it is certainly so from the time of his mother's death. Just before the vigil at the *asile*, the caretaker explains to Meursault the need to bury corpses more quickly here than in Paris where it is cooler. His wife, understandably, protests at the unsuitable nature of the discussion, given Meursault's present circumstances. Meursault tells us: 'J'étais intervenu pour dire: "Mais non. Mais non." Je trouvais ce qu'il racontait juste et intéressant' (I.I, 16) He makes the same comment concerning Raymond's unsavoury conversation: 'Je trouve que ce qu'il dit est intéressant' (I.III, 47–8). And it is above all to Raymond and his affairs that Meursault accords a place of prime importance in his narrative. More important, Raymond is the only human being with whom Meursault becomes really involved. It is worth tracing the major stages marking his progressive and ultimately fatal involvement.

Stage 1: Raymond relates to Meursault, boastfully as always, his fight with the man on the tram. He proceeds to give a detailed and coloured account of his relationship with his Arab mistress. The violence and cruelty underlying his nature and behaviour emerge clearly. Meursault is at this point an interested but uninvolved listener (I.III, 48–53).

Stage 2: Bent on revenge for her alleged unfaithfulness, Raymond resolves to write a letter to his mistress, the content of which is resumed in 'avec des coups de pied et en même temps des choses à la faire regretter', and the intention of which is resumed in 'Après, quand elle reviendrait, il coucherait avec elle et "juste au moment de finir" il lui cracherait à la figure et il la mettrait dehors.' The composition of this letter is apparently beyond Raymond's powers of literacy. He asks Meursault to write it for him. Meursault, co-operative as ever, agrees to do so and obviously performs his task with some degree of skill. He reads his letter aloud to Raymond: 'Il a été tout à fait content. Il m'a dit: "Je savais bien que tu connaissais bien la vie".' Meursault at this point remains uninvolved in a direct sense. But his writing of the letter and his reading it aloud imply, however detached he apparently remains, a degree of vicarious involvement (I.III, 54).

Stage 3: Raymond's mistress has rejoined him. The content of the letter written by Meursault is carried out in practice. There is a violent quarrel which spills out on to the landing of the apartment building. Raymond beats his mistress. A policeman arrives, hits Raymond and humiliates him. Meursault and Marie, with other neighbours, watch these events. Meursault at this point, vicariously though not directly implicated in the matter, is a somewhat involved observer (I.IV, 59–61).

Stage 4: Raymond telephones Meursault and informs him he has been followed by a group of Arabs, including his mistress's brother. He asks Meursault to tell him if he sees the Arabs near the house. Meursault complies. At this point Meursault has been asked to involve himself directly, to however small a degree, in the Raymond affair. He is willing to do so (I.V, 67–8).

Stage 5: The group of Arabs watch Raymond, Meursault and Marie silently as they make their way to Masson's beach-hut. They do not follow them. Meursault has now been involved in a direct encounter with the Arabs, but one which, for the moment, is of no consequence (I.VI, 79).

Stage 6: Raymond, Masson and Meursault walk along the beach. They meet two Arabs. Raymond and Masson 'take' one each and assault them. Meursault stands by: ' "Toi, Meursault, s'il en arrive un autre, il est pour toi". J'ai dit: "Oui".' Raymond's Arab draws a knife, Meursault cries out in warning but Raymond's arm and mouth are cut. The Arabs withdraw. In this three to two situation Meursault is the least involved. But his involvement is nonetheless direct and considerable (I.VI, 86–7).

Stage 7: Raymond, having received medical treatment, wishes to return along the beach alone. He angrily rejects Masson's and Meursault's offers to accompany him. But Meursault goes with him. They encounter the two Arabs. Raymond draws a revolver. Meursault, attempting to calm him, takes it from him. The four stare at one another for a long time. The Arabs withdraw. The relationship is now two to two. Meursault is a more directly involved participant in a tense, potentially violent situation (I.VI, 88–91).

Stage 8: Meursault, the revolver in his pocket, walks along the beach, alone. He meets the Arab, alone. The situation is one to one. Meursault kills the Arab. The gradual progress from his initial fascination with Raymond to the killing of the Arab is complete. He is now fully involved; he has become both the instrument and the embodiment of violence and death (I.VI, 91–5).

The eight stages described above are, of course, interwoven into the rest of the narrative content of Part 1. But when we isolate them and then juxtapose them in the above manner a striking series of patterns emerge. We note throughout each stage a gradual but persistent and accelerating increase in Meursault's personal involvement in these violent or potentially violent situations. Within this dramatic development of events Meursault moves through the roles of listener, observer, vicarious participant, direct and increasingly important direct participant to principal actor. As the events unfold one by one, they, and Meursault within them, move towards an inevitable climax and catharsis. The focus narrows consistently; gradually at first, then sharply. In Chapters III, IV and V, Meursault's movement towards the final violent scene is relatively slow. In Chapter VI the pace quickens, violent encounter follows violent encounter with increasing rapidity. Within the narrative the tension builds to an unbearable pitch, then breaks.

It is not just within the narrative that the tension builds. It builds in Meursault too. Violence once unleashed in him must be fulfilled. It must end with death, the death of the Arab, a symbolic prefiguration of his own death and that of all mankind.

Meursault is not satisfied with half-measures. Masson withdraws after the first encounter; the Arabs withdraw after each of the first two encounters; Raymond, apparently sated after the second encounter, withdraws. But the situation is unresolved, the tension remains. Where Meursault is concerned, none of these encounters has achieved a satisfactory climax, a consummation which will release him from the now unbearable tension within him. Possessed now by the violence which step by step has grown within him, he is driven to consummate the violence, to kill the Arab, and thus achieve release. Symbolically, the act of murder contains within it a demonstration of the ambivalence of his nature in the face of death in an absurd world; it is at once an expression of his rage at an order of creation which gives him precious life only to snatch it away again in death, and an expression of his innate compulsion to embrace that death. It is an absurd act.

The four elements repeatedly referred to in this section again are present here: Meursault, another human presence, nature and death. Again, combined, they reveal the basis of his character. The Arab remains a distant, shadowy figure; the narrative never accords him the flesh and blood, the full presence of a living being. Meursault remains impervious to his humanity. But the impact of the natural world is omnipresent within him; the narrative accords it, in full measure, the powerful description of a living force.

Chance plays its part throughout Part I and chance plays its part in bringing about this confrontation. But the result is not the work of chance but of necessity. For this confrontation between Meursault, the Arab and nature is the embodiment of the absurd divorce which there is between human existence and the natural world. Now inescapably involved in the confrontation of these irreconcilables, Meursault is forced to choose, and the choice he makes, albeit subconsciously, means that the natural world prevails and human life is destroyed. Throughout Part I Camus has prepared us for the fact that the choice Meursault must make is chiefly dependent not upon chance or circumstance but upon his character.

4. *Attitudes*

Car si j'essaie de saisir ce moi dont je m'assure, si j'essaie de le résumer et de le définir, il n'est plus qu'une eau qui coule entre mes doigts. . . . Entre la certitude que j'ai de mon existence et le contenu que j'essaie de donner à cette assurance le fossé ne sera jamais comblé. Pour toujours je serai étranger à moi-même. (Le Mythe de Sisyphe)

Meursault does not like questions. Questions demand answers and answers are, by their very nature, some form of definition, of interpretation, of explanation. When Meursault finally embarks upon a recreation of his past experience, his account takes the form of a description of events and behaviour. There is no conscious attempt at defining, interpreting or explaining them. On the contrary, Meursault the self-aware character-narrator shares with his earlier self, the as yet unaware subject of the narration, a marked tendency to shun any such exercise.

Meursault seeks *le mot juste*; if he cannot find it he prefers no words at all. This characteristic renders him untypical of the majority of people with whom he comes into contact and, whether it be a question of his relationship with his mother or of the meaning of being, is at the root of his 'differentness' from them. Thus we infer a certain sympathy in him for those who cannot understand things or express themselves. He enjoys Emmanuel's company (I.IV, 57). He enjoys Masson's company (I.IV, 82). He enjoys Céleste's company (II.III, 145). And at the end of Celeste's testimony, Meursault avows a positive emotional reaction to another human being and replies in kind—'Moi, je n'ai rien dit, je n'ai fait aucun geste'—to the wealth of feeling and goodwill which Céleste clearly feels but simply cannot articulate.

All these episodes are tinged with a humour indulged in by the narrator Meursault at the expense of his companions who seem a trifle slow or who make fools of themselves. But it is a gentle, sympathetic humour, quite without malice. Meursault approves of his minor comic victims. In a way, taking Meursault and these three minor figures together, we may see a composite prototype of Grand in *La Peste*, the good, gentle Grand whose novel will never be written because he can never get the right words, nor put words in the right order to express all that he feels.

Marie is bewildered at Meursault's—in her eyes—inconsistent attitude towards her:

> Le soir, Marie est venue me chercher et m'a demandé si je voulais me marier avec elle. J'ai dit que cela m'était égal et que nous pourrions le faire si elle le voulait. Elle a voulu savoir alors si je l'aimais. J'ai répondu comme je l'avais déjà fait une fois, que cela ne signifiait rien mais que sans doute je ne l'aimais pas. 'Pourquoi m'épouser alors?' a-t-elle dit. Je lui ai expliqué que cela n'avait aucune importance et que si elle le désirait, nous pouvions nous marier.   (I.V, 69)

But his attitude is consistent and its reason is to be found in his refusal to accept a word which commits him to the acceptance of an experience he cannot measure or define. In his relationship with Marie—and elsewhere—he is agreeably positive when he can be sure of his grounds, but obstinately negative when no such grounds exist. *Marriage* is, on one level, a social phenomenon, a describable and definable formal process. It is not important to him but at least he knows what it means, so he is willing to accept it. But *love*, even should it exist, is a word of a quite different order. It claims to define an experience which he can neither identify nor measure. He prefers therefore to deny it, for that is the truth as he knows it. The same attitude underlies the limited degree of his willingness to define his relationship with his mother—an attitude which, in this instance, causes him a great deal of trouble. We know that he thinks about and refers a good deal to his mother, that she said a number of things which he admires and approves of, and that he would have preferred it had she not died. In short, as far as we or he can judge, their relationship was based upon some degree of respect and affection. It seems equally misjudged to try to prove either that he cared nothing for her, or that he loved her deeply. He does not know, he cannot define the terms, and therefore will not commit himself to any qualitative or quantitative evaluation of his feelings. Both the *avocat* and the *juge d'instruction* ask Meursault if he loves his mother. His answers on both occasions indicate a refusal to give any but the most banal and noncommittal of replies (II.I, 102 and 105). The question and the nature of the answers Meursault gives inform the whole of the examination and lead to the dramatic (and fatuous) accusation: '—j'accuse cet homme d'avoir enterré une mère avec un coeur de criminel' (II.III, 150).

Meursault and his accusers think and talk constantly at cross purposes. Whatever 'interpretation' they choose to give to his replies and attitude, they are, in essence, based upon his desire to tell the truth and only the truth as far as he is able concerning his feelings, and upon a profound respect for language, his only (inadequate) means of conveying that truth.

At every level Meursault encounters people bent on attempting to interpret and modify his behaviour, his character and his life by imposing upon them a series of glib definitions. They tell him what he should do, what he should think and feel; they interpret for him the significance of his experience, explain to him the meaning of his life. The director and the caretaker of the *asile* feel sure he will want to see his mother's corpse. Marie feels he ought to love her. His boss feels he ought to be ambitious. The *juge d'instruction* feels he should accept his guilt in the eyes of the law and in the eyes of God, and, prostrating himself before them, ask for their mercy and forgiveness. The *aumônier* begs him to see the truth of the Christian message, to submit himself to the view of the human condition contained therein. To all of them Meursault's response is uniformly negative and the tone of the narrative indicates that for a long time, as he moves from description to description of these various negative responses, the character-narrator's sense of self-control and sense of humour do not desert him. But they finally do so to be replaced by a passionate disavowal of everything he is not and what his life has not been, and an equally passionate avowal of what he is and what his life has been.

The smallest detail of conventional behaviour, of a formal response to any given circumstance, implies, albeit unconsciously, the acceptance of the fact that existence has a meaning, and the notion that there is a 'proper' way of reacting to it. Meursault resists such a code of conduct even when the demands of convention happen to coincide with the promptings of his instinct. For example, his immediate desire, on arriving at the *asile*, is to see his mother's corpse (I.I, 11). As he waits before doing so, the concierge prattles on and the director, when he arrives, goes through all the proper motions, displays all the proper sentiments. This unctuous man has made all the necessary arrangements, understands perfectly why Meursault felt constrained to place his mother in the *asile*, has fulfilled the last wishes of Madame Meursault by ordering a religious burial, has gone to the trouble of removing the body to the morgue so as not to upset the other inmates, and feels sure that Meursault would like to see his mother's body. Meursault makes no reply but when, soon afterwards, the caretaker offers to take the lid off the coffin Meursault indicates clearly that he has no wish to see the corpse (I.I, 11–14). He has changed his mind. He has done so because the mechanistic, professionally self-conscious and ultimately meaningless behaviour patterns of the director have come to impose themselves upon his own initially spontaneous impulse. The director cares nothing for this death, nor, by implication, any other; he goes through the motions of a vulgar, empty ritual. Meursault dissociates himself from his posturings. The sardonic and ironic tone of the narrative indicates that he finds them as distasteful as he finds them grotesquely amusing.

Thus not only in the language they use but also in the patterns of behaviour they adopt—and the two are closely linked—do so many of the people Meursault encounters attempt to give significance to the lives they lead. The tone of detachment, of sardonic and at times cruel humour which informs so much of the narrative is the result of Meursault's reaction to an observation of their antics.

The limping Pérez is determined to observe the conventions and pay his last respects to his 'fiancée'; he follows the funeral procession, but, given his age and infirmity, is unable to keep up with it. In order to do so he takes several short-cuts across the fields (I.I, 30). The more one visualizes the scene, the more incongruous and ridiculous it becomes. Faced with the death of Madame Meursault, a mirror of his own solitude and impending death, the old man struggles manfully to keep up appearances. But his pathetic attempts to express his bereavement through observing a convention he is no longer able to fulfil with dignity are ludicrous. In a deadpan, laconic way Meursault exploits quite mercilessly his misery and his absurdity.

He does the same with Salamano. When Salamano finally loses his dog—an animal he insults, persecutes and beats, but which is the only thing in life he has left to cling to—he turns to Meursault, his sympathetic listener, for advice. Meursault's response is curt and cruel (I.IV, 65). He cannot resist turning the knife, reminding himself, his reader and, at times, his associates of the stark ultimate reality of solitude and death, a reality we do all in our power to conceal from ourselves. For Pascal's *libertin*, the only escape from such a reality is a metaphysical leap into the consolation of faith; for Camus's Meursault, despite certain promptings to the contrary, there is no such hope.

If the pathos of characters such as Salamano and Pérez bring out a cruel streak in Meursault, the rantings of the *juge d'instruction*, the pleadings of the *aumônier*, and the grounds upon which both are based, arouse in him feelings of distaste, contempt and finally anger. For Meursault, the view of life held by both of them is at once cringing and arrogant in its assumptions.

The description of the interview with the *juge d'instruction* (II.I, 103–9) is particularly interesting. At the onset of the interview the senior representative of law and order is courteous and self-controlled. But faced with the laconic and unrevealing nature of Meursault's replies to questions concerning his relationship with his mother and his firing of the four shots, unable to penetrate the mind of this obstinate criminal, he loses his composure and apparently goes berserk. He takes on the characteristics of a ranting hot-gospeller. Brandishing a crucifix in Meursault's face, he launches into a tirade on the subject of his own religious convictions, on his belief that the mercy of God is infinite, that Christ died for all men, that in our guilt we must seek his forgiveness. He is convinced that in their heart of hearts all men, including Meursault, cannot fail to believe in God, to accept the Christian message. In the face of this passionate outburst Meursault remains unmoved. The eloquence, the rhetoric, the burning faith of the *juge* have no apparent effect upon him. Not only does he remain an obstinate non-believer, he is simply not interested in the matter. Thus Meursault's cool, detached, faintly amused attitude is played off against the judge's uncontrolled behaviour.

Now this encounter may have taken place in the manner Meursault describes, but it seems hardly likely. It seems more probable that, in tone and form at least, it is a fiction within the fiction. The *juge* is a caricature, a wildly exaggerated amalgam of certain human attitudes and social, moral and religious beliefs. He and they are the butt of Camus's contempt and ridicule. And this is the hub of the matter. Camus's intention, achieved as always through the medium of his character-narrator, is to bring into focus in this important exchange the various interdependent strata of human activity and belief which combine in a view of the human condition within which Meursault must, on every count, stand condemned.

The interview with the *juge d'instruction* is a caricatural pre-enactment of the trial and condemnation of Meursault. The *juge*, emotional, irrational, arrogantly sure of himself and the truth of his beliefs, representative of a legal system which assumes the right to judge all men and to condemn them to death, imbued with a religious faith which demands that all men accept their guilt and seek forgiveness from above, is the embodiment of the social, moral and religious values underlying the society which judges and condemns Meursault. These values are all of a piece and Meursault will have no part of them. In his nature and in his attitude he remains a stranger to them.

Thus throughout Part II Camus uses Meursault as the vehicle of his satire of certain human assumptions. The assumption underlying all other assumptions is that human life has a meaning and significance beyond itself; and Christianity is the specific source of this belief. The *juge* speaks for all men who subscribe to that particular system of belief—and for many who do not—when he cries incredulously: 'Voulez-vous . . . que ma vie n'ait pas de sens?' (II.I, 108) Camus uses Meursault's foreign presence, in a society smugly convinced that its values and practices are the embodiment of absolute truth, to shake the foundations of its every assumption.

In his encounter with the *aumônier* (II.VI, 177–87) Meursault, once more hounded by an alien world attempting persistently to impose its values and beliefs upon him, finally loses patience and control and passionately avows his rejection of all 'truths' other than the only truth he knows, that of his own existence. Above all, he rejects Christianity; he rejects the notion of his own guilt and need for forgiveness which it implies; he rejects its promise of eternal life, a promise he would like to believe in, but cannot. He accepts only his life as it has been, and still is, and the certainty of death and absolute extinction now awaiting him.

In the light of this is seems paradoxical that his final words—when *his* awareness of the conflict within him between his desire to live again, for ever, and the opposing fact of his imminent death is at its most intense—should reflect an image of the Crucifixion:

> Pour que tout soit consommé, pour que je me sente moins seul, il me restait à souhaiter qu'il y ait beaucoup de spectateurs le jour de mon exécution et qu'ils m'accueillent avec des cris de haine.   (II.VI, 188)

The Christ alluded to in these words is not Christ the God but Christ the man, who simply lived and died. The attitude towards him conveyed by the last sentence of *L'Etranger* is reflected in a statement made later by Camus:

> J'admire la façon dont il a vécu, dont il est mort. Mon manque d'imagination m'interdit de le suivre plus loin.   (*Le Monde*, 31 August 1956)

One thing is clear from this: Camus does not accept the divinity of Christ. Yet here, as elsewhere in his work, Camus is haunted by the myth of Christ. It is perhaps not possible to define precisely the reason for this. What aspects of the figure of Christ attract him? Is it his innocence, his outspokenness, his love of the truth as he sees it and his bearing witness to it, his strength and dignity in the face of death? Whatever the answer, Camus chooses to put finally into the mouth of his character-narrator the words which evoke irresistibly the last moments of Christ.

Christ faces death with dignity and acceptance. He is executed in a public place. The crowd greets him with cries of hatred for, dying there before them on the cross, he is the embodiment of the human condition and the ultimate destiny of all men, a destiny which they hate and fear. He accepts to carry the burden of their fears; as he does so, in their very rejection of him, he is united to them. Hence Meursault's death and his acceptance of it. He is, as Camus calls him, 'le seul Christ que nous méritions' (8 January 1955).

5. Conclusion

Donner une forme à ce qui n'en a pas, c'est le but de toute œuvre. Il n'y a pas seulement création mais correction. (Camus, *Carnets 1942–51*)

Reading *L'Etranger* is a shock and a pleasure.

It is a shock, a sustained series of shocks, because through the medium of his character-narrator Meursault, Camus creates in us a deep disquiet concerning the foundations and assumptions of our familiar world. Whether we like Meursault or not, agree with him or not, approve of him or not, find his behaviour immoral or not, he forces us to question our every assumption: our use of language, our habits, our relationships with others, the very substance, shape and purpose of our existence. His function is to destroy our complacency. Meursault moves from a peaceful state of unawareness of his situation to an apprehension and awareness of the absurdity of the world as he sees it. In reading *L'Etranger* we share this apprehension and awareness.

But it is also a pleasure, a considerable pleasure, because Camus's art, shared within the fiction by his character-narrator, is an art whereby that which threatens formlessness is given form, that which threatens meaninglessness is given meaning, that which threatens to dominate us is dominated. For the characteristics of the narrative technique of *L'Etranger*, its measure, its balance, its economy and understatement, its coolness and irony, are the characteristics of the author who creates it, as they are those of his character-narrator. The suitability of form to content is perfect. They are indivisibly at one. The author and his character are determined to face squarely the implications of the absurd world and, through the discipline of their art, to triumph over it. The whole tension of the book and much of the pleasure we experience in reading it reside in the confrontation and ultimate fusion of the *démesure* of Meursault's destiny and the *mesure* of the language in which he describes it. Camus's *L'Etranger* is indeed '*une œuvre classique, une œuvre d'ordre, composée à propos de l'absurde et contre l'absurde.*'

Biographical Note (1913–43)

1913   Albert Camus is born on 7 November in Mondovi, Algeria, the second child (he has an elder brother, Lucien) of Lucien and Catherine (*née* Sintès) Camus. His father, of Alsatian stock (the family having settled in Algeria in 1871), works as cellarman in a wine merchant's. His mother's family comes from Majorca.

1914   Camus's father is killed in the Battle of the Marne. The family moves to Belcourt, a working-class district of Algiers. Family circumstances are difficult and impoverished; his mother, who is almost stone deaf and seldom speaks, works as a charwoman. She, the two young boys, Camus's grandmother and an invalid uncle live in a two-room flat.

1918   Camus goes to the *école communale* in Belcourt where he is to stay till 1923. One of his teachers, Louis Germain, takes a special interest in him, gives him extra tuition and eventually enters him for various scholarships for the *lycées* and colleges.

1923   Camus wins a scholarship to the *Lycée d'Alger* where he is to stay till 1930.

1928   Beginning this year and for the next two seasons Camus plays in goal for the soccer club *Racing-Universitaire d'Alger*.

1930   Camus passes his *baccalauréat* but his formal studies are interrupted by the first of a series of attacks of tuberculosis. He is forced to leave his crowded home and live with an uncle, a butcher by trade, an avid reader and intellectual by inclination. He introduces Camus to the works of Gide. For some months, in convalescence, Camus leads an independent life, living in various parts of Algiers.

1932   Camus continues his studies in Lettres Supérieures. Amongst his teachers is Jean Grenier, whom he is to meet again later at University. The work and the personality of this philosopher and essayist are to have a deep and lasting effect on Camus's thinking. The review *Sud* publishes four articles by Camus: *Un Nouveau Verlaine, Jehan Rictus, Essai sur la Musique, La Philosophie du Siècle*.

1933   Soon after Hitler's rise to power on 30 January Camus becomes an active member of the Mouvement Antifasciste Amsterdam-Pleyel founded by Henri Barbusse and Romain Rolland. Camus is reading Proust at this time and in this year Jean Grenier's *Les Iles* is published: a collection of short essays, poetic, ironic, sceptical in tone, it deals with the problems of existence and, throughout his life, Camus continues to stress his indebtedness to it.

1934   Camus's first marriage, which ends in divorce two years later. Towards the end of the year Camus joins the Communist Party. In 1955 he claims, in a letter to Roger Quilliot, that he left the Party the following year, 1935, as a result of the visit of Laval to Moscow which led to the Communist Party withdrawing much of its support for the demands of the Arab population. However, friends of Camus suggest that he remained a member of the Party until the latter stages of 1937 when a row broke out between the Communist Party and the Parti du Peuple algérien de Messali Hadj, which believed the Communists to be chiefly responsible for the repression suffered by the Arabs; they claim that Camus resigned at this point. Whichever date is correct, it is clear that Camus's membership of the Communist Party is brought to an end by what he believes to be their betrayal of the Arab population; Camus himself is at this time and for years to come active in his support for betterment in the conditions governing the lives of the Arabs.

1935   Camus begins to write *L'Envers et l'endroit*. At this time he is pursuing his studies in philosophy at the Faculté d'Alger, where Grenier is now teaching. To make a living he takes various jobs, such as salesman of spare parts for motorcars, clerk in the préfecture and reporter for the meteorological service in the Faculté.

1936   Camus completes his thesis for the *diplôme d'études supérieures de philosophie*; its title is *Métaphysique chrétienne et néoplatonisme*. He is reading in particular Epictetus, Pascal, Kierkegaard, Gide and Malraux. (Malraux has by now published *La Voie royale*, *Les Conquérants*, *La Condition humaine* and *Le Temps du mépris* and, through him, Camus is greatly attracted to the notion of the *écrivain engagé*.) In June, Camus travels in central Europe. On his return to Algiers with several friends Camus takes charge of the Maison de la Culture (controlled by the Communist Party) and founds the Théâtre du Travail. The aim of this troupe is to bring together young revolutionary intellectuals, scholars, students, all more or less influenced by Marxism; to unite artists, painters, sculptors, workers, petits-bourgeois, all of them actively involved in political movements. It is to be a revolutionary theatre, a popular theatre, but not a totalitarian theatre; its precise aims are to exploit the artistic value of popular literature and to show that art can sometimes come out of its ivory tower. Amongst its early presentations are: Camus's adaptation of Malraux's *Le Temps du mépris*, Aeschylus's *Prometheus Bound (Le Prométhée enchaîné)*, Gorki's *The Lower Depths (Bas-fonds)*, Ben Jonson's *Epicoene, or The Silent Woman (La Femme silencieuse)*, and, on 24 March 1937, for the centenary of the death of Pushkin, *Don Juan*, Camus himself playing the title role. During the first year of life of the Théâtre du Travail, Camus with several colleagues creates *Révolte dans les Asturies*, a work of propaganda commemorating the Spanish workers' insurrection in 1934. Commitment to the cause of Spanish republicanism is clear enough and the mayor of Algiers does not allow the play to be performed.

1937 As a result of Camus's quarrel with the Communist Party, the Théâtre du Travail is disbanded. However, its members quickly come together again under the name of the Théâtre de l'Equipe. In its manifesto of October 1937 it claims to be a young theatre, seeking in the works it presents truth and simplicity, violence and cruelty. And so it will turn to those periods where love of life is mingled with despair in living: ancient Greece (Aeschylus and Aristophanes), Elizabethan England (Marlowe, Shakespeare), Spain (de Rojas, Calderon, Cervantes), America (Faulkner), and contemporary French literature (Claudel, Malraux) The Théâtre de l'Equipe is to be without political or religious *parti pris*; a spirit of freedom and youthfulness is to reign.

Camus is engaged as an actor by Radio-Alger. He refuses a teaching post in the Collège de Sidi-Bel-Abbès. Because of his poor health he is not allowed to sit for the *agrégation de philosophie*.

L'Envers et l'endroit is published in May. He is working on *Noces* and on *La Mort heureuse*, an unfinished novel only recently published (1971). He takes a post as a journalist on the newspaper *Alger Républicain*, founded by Pascal Pia. His commitments are numerous and varied: collecting local news items, writing editorials, the literary column, and above all reporting and commenting on political trials and debates in Algeria. In 1938 he contributes some 25 articles, in 1939 some 80; in the latter part of 1939 he also contributes a number of articles to the *Soir Républicain*, mostly on the subject of the second world war, some of them under the pen name of Jean Mersault.

1938   Camus writes *Caligula*, considers writing an essay on the absurd, begins to make notes which he will use when writing *L'Etranger*. He is reading Nietzsche (*Human, All Too Human, The Twilight of the Gods*) and Kierkegaard (*The Sickness unto Death*). Publication of Malraux's *L'Espoir* and Sartre's *La Nausée*. Camus is very appreciative of Sartre's novel but criticizes the author for basing his conception of the tragedy of existence solely upon a presentation of human ugliness. He writes in *Alger Républicain* on 20 October 1938: 'Et le héros de M. Sartre n'a peut-être pas fourni le vrai sens de son angoisse lorsqu'il insiste sur ce qui lui répugne dans l'homme, au lieu de fonder sur certaines de ses grandeurs des raisons de désespérer.'

1939   *Noces* is published in May. Throughout the first half of June, Camus presents in *Alger Républicain* a long, searching report on Kabylia, a region of Algeria to the east of Algiers. He contrasts the beauty of the country with the miserable and poverty-stricken conditions of the people who live there. He meets Malraux and reads Sartre's recently published *Le Mur*. The international situation prevents him from going on an intended trip to Greece. On the outbreak of the second world war, Camus attempts 'par solidarité' to join the army. He is refused on grounds of ill health.

1940   Camus marries for the second time; his wife, Francine Faure, comes from Oran. By 10 January the newspaper *Alger Républicain*, because of its editors' refusal to comply with the wishes of the censors, has closed down. Camus, denied employment and at odds with official policies, leaves Algeria. He takes a job with the newspaper *Paris-Soir*. In May *L'Etranger* is completed. That same month the German invasion takes place and Camus moves to Clermont-Ferrand; he continues to work for *Paris-Soir* until December. He completes the first part of *Le Mythe de Sisyphe* in September. He moves to Lyon in October.

1941   In January he returns to Oran in Algeria. He takes employment in a private school where most of the children are Jewish. In February he completes *Le Mythe de Sisyphe*. Having read and been very impressed by Melville's *Moby Dick* ('l'un des mythes les plus bouleversants qu'on ait jamais imaginés sur le combat de l'homme juste contre la création et le créateur d'abord, puis contre ses semblables et contre lui-même'), he begins work on *La Peste*. He is also reading Tolstoy, Marcus Aurelius, de Sade. On 19 December the Nazis shoot Gabriel Péri, one of the leaders of the French Communist Party, and Camus decides to join the Resistance.

1942   By now Camus is working for the clandestine newspaper *Combat*. He suffers a serious attack of tuberculosis, is forced to suspend his activities and go to convalesce in Le Forez, in the Lyon area. He intends to rejoin his wife, Francine, who is still in Algeria, but the Allied landing in Algeria and Morocco on 8 November prevents the reunion; the couple remain separated and unable to communicate until the Liberation (August 1944). He is reading Melville, Defoe, Cervantes, Balzac, Mme de Lafayette, Kierkegaard and Spinoza.

In July *L'Etranger* is published by Gallimard. *Le Mythe de Sisyphe* appears later the same year.

1943   The Resistance movements *Franc-tireur*, *Combat* and *Libération* join forces; the staff of *Combat* base themselves in Paris where Camus lives in Gide's flat. He completes the first draft of his play *Le Malentendu* (first performed 1944). He writes the first of four *Lettres à un ami allemand*, published clandestinely. He takes a job as proof-reader for Gallimard. He writes and has published *L'Intelligence et l'échafaud*.

Select Critical Bibliography

A number of the works listed below contain quite extensive critical bibliographies. I refer you in particular to:

Camus: a bibliography, compiled and edited by Robert F. Roeming (Madison, Milwaukee, University of Wisconsin Press and London, 1968).

Calepins de bibliographie, Camus no. 1, essai de bibliographie des études en langue française consacrées à Albert Camus by Brian T. Fitch and Peter C. Hoy (*Lettres modernes*, 1969). (See also below: Fitch, B. T.)

Camus devant la critique anglo-saxonne. Tests compiled and presented by J. H. Matthews (*Revue des lettres modernes* 64–6, 1961).

General studies

Brée, G., *Camus* (New Jersey, Rutgers University Press 1959).

Brée, G. (ed.), *Camus: a collection of critical essays* (Englewood Cliffs, NJ, Prentice-Hall 1962).

Cruickshank, J., *Albert Camus and the literature of revolt* (London, OUP 1959).

Gadourek, C., *Les Innocents et les coupables* (La Haye, Mouton 1963).

Ginestier, P., *La Pensée de Camus* (Paris, Bordas 1964).

Grenier, J., *Albert Camus (Souvenirs)* (Paris, Gallimard 1968).

King, A., *Camus* (London and Edinburgh, Oliver and Boyd 1964).

Nguyen-Van-Huey, P., *La Métaphysique du bonheur chez Albert Camus* (Neuchâtel, La Baconnière 1962).

O'Brien, C. C., *Camus* (London, Fontana 1970).

Onimus, J., *Camus* (Bruges, Les Ecrivains devant Dieu 1965).

Quilliot, R., *La Mer et les prisons, essai sur Camus* (Paris, Gallimard, 1956, 2nd rev. and cor. edn. 1970).

Simon P-H. *et al.*, *Camus* (Paris, Hachette 1964).

Thody, P., *Camus 1913–1960* (London, Hamish Hamilton 1964).

Books on 'L'Etranger':

Barrier, M.-G., *L'Art du récit dans L'Etranger d'Albert Camus* (Paris, Nizet 1962).

Castex, P.-G., *Albert Camus et L'Etranger* (Paris, Corti 1965).

Champigny, R., *Sur un Héros paien* (Paris, Gallimard 1959).

Fitch, B. T., *Narrateur et narration dans L'Etranger d'Albert Camus* (Paris, Minard, 2nd rev. edn. 1968).

Fitch, B. T. *et al.*, *Autour de L'Etranger* (*Revue des lettres modernes* 170–74, Paris 1968).

Fitch, B. T., *L'Etranger d'Albert Camus; un texte, ses lecteurs, leurs lectures* (Paris, Librairie Larousse 1972). Contains an excellent critical bibliography, with summaries, of books and articles in English and French devoted to *L'Etranger*.

Pingaud, B., *L'Etranger de Camus* (Paris, Hachette 1971).

Rey, P.-L., *L'Etranger, Camus* (Paris, Hatier, 1970).

Critical essays on 'L'Etranger':

Sartre, J.-P., *Explication de L'Etranger*. This indispensable essay was first published in *Cahiers du Sud*, February 1943; it is contained in Sartre's *Situations 1* (Gallimard 1947, pp. 99–121), and in abbreviated form in *Les Critiques de notre temps et Camus* (see below). An English version is available in Germaine Brée's edition of critical essays: *Camus* (see above).

Lévi-Valensi, Jacqueline *et al.*, *Les Critiques de notre temps et Camus* (Paris, Garnier 1970). In this excellent collection of critical essays the following, as well as the abridged version of Sartre's essay, are all of great use and interest: Jean Grenier, 'Une œuvre, un homme'; Nathalie Sarraute, 'La psychologie dans *L'Etranger*'; Roland Barthes, '*L'Etranger*, roman solaire'; Alain Robbe-Grillet, 'Nature, humanisme, tragédie'; Pierre-Georges Castex, 'L'art de l'écrivain'.